TEXT AND PERFORMANCE

General Editor: Michael Scott

The series is designed to introduce sixth-form and under-graduate students to the themes, continuing vitality and performance of major dramatic works. The attention given to production aspects is an element of special importance, responding to the invigoration given to literary study by the work of leading contemporary critics.

The prime aim is to present each play as a vital experience in the mind of the reader – achieved by analysis of the text in relation to its themes and theatricality. Emphasis is accordingly placed on the relevance of the work to the modern reader and the world of today. At the same time, traditional views are presented and appraised, forming the basis from which a creative response to the text can develop.

In each volume, Part One: *Text* discusses certain themes or problems, the reader being encouraged to gain a stronger perception both of the inherent character of the work and also of variations in interpreting it. Part Two: *Performance* examines the ways in which these themes or problems have been handled in modern productions, and the approaches and techniques employed to enhance the play's accessibility to modern audiences.

A synopsis of the play is given and an outline of its major sources, and a concluding Reading List offers guidance to the student's independent study of the work.

PUBLISHED

ROMEO AND JULIET

Text and Performance

PETER HOLDING

MACMILLAN

First published 1992 by
MACMILLAN EDUCATION LTD
Houndmills, Basingstoke, Hampshire RG21 2XS
and London
Companies and representatives
throughout the world

ISBN 0–333–51912–4

A catalogue record for this book is available
from the British Library.

Typeset by Footnote Graphics,
Warminster, Wiltshire

Printed in Hong Kong

CONTENTS

TO EDITH

ACKNOWLEDGEMENTS

All quotations from *Romeo and Juliet* are taken from the New Penguin Shakespeare edition (1967), edited by T. J. B. Spencer.

Other quotations from Shakespeare are from *The Complete Works* (1951), edited by Peter Alexander.

I express sincere thanks to Dr. Marian J. Pringle, Senior Librarian, and her staff at The Shakespeare Centre, Stratford-upon-Avon for their endless patience and assistance with the promptbooks and production materials for all of the RSC productions.

I wish also to thank Professor Ejner Jensen, of the University of Michigan, and Professor Stanley Wells, of the Shakespeare Institute, University of Birmingham, who both helped to shape my thinking on this play and all matters Shakespearian.

GENERAL EDITOR'S PREFACE

For many years a mutual suspicion existed between the theatre director and the literary critic of drama. Although in the first half of the century there were important exceptions, such was the rule. A radical change of attitude, however, has taken place over the last thirty years. Critics and directors now increasingly recognise the significance of each other's work and acknowledge their growing awareness of inter-dependence. Both interpret the same text, but do so according to their different situations and functions. Without the direc-tor, the designer and the actor, a play's existence is only partial. They revitalise the text with action, enabling the drama to live fully at each performance. The academic critic investigates the script to elucidate its textual problems, under-stand its conventions and discover how it operates. He may also propose his view of the work, expounding what he considers to be its significance.

Dramatic texts belong therefore to theatre and to literature. The aim of the 'Text and Performance' series is to achieve a fuller recognition of how both enhance our enjoyment of the play. Each volume follows the same basic pattern. Part One provides a critical introduction to the play under discussion, using the techniques and criteria of the literary critic in examining the manner in which the work operates through language, imagery and action. Part Two takes the enquiry further into the play's theatricality by focusing on selected productions of recent times so as to illustrate points of contrast and comparison in the interpretation of different directors and actors, and to demonstrate how the drama has worked on the modern stage. In this way the series seeks to provide a lively and informative introduction to major plays in their text and performance.

MICHAEL SCOTT

PLOT SYNOPSIS AND SOURCES

In Verona an old feud breaks out between two families, the Capulets and the Montagues. The Prince, Escalus, unable to control the two parties, threatens death to anyone who again disturbs the peace. Romeo, son to Montague, reveals his infatuation for Rosaline and is teased for his romantic excesses by his friends Benvolio and Mercutio. By chance the three learn that Capulet intends to have a feast and they decide to attend, masked and uninvited. During the course of the festivities Romeo sees Juliet, the only child of Capulet and the two fall instantly in love. Despite the danger, Romeo gains access to the garden of Juliet's house and the two declare their love for one another, separated by the height of the balcony at which Juliet stands. The next day, with the assistance of Juliet's nurse and their confessor, Friar Laurence, the two are secretly married. Soon after Romeo meets Juliet's cousin Tybalt, who challenges him to a duel. He declines but Mercutio accepts the challenge in his place. In an attempt to stop the fight Romeo steps in between the two and Mercutio is killed in the confusion. Romeo avenges the death by killing Tybalt and must then go into hiding. The Prince banishes Romeo, who takes the Friar's advice and goes to Mantua. After being told by her father that she must marry Paris, a relative of the Prince, Juliet goes in despair to Friar Laurence. The Friar gives her a sleeping potion which mimics death. He plans that after she is buried she will revive and secretly be reunited with Romeo. The Friar sends a message to Romeo which is delayed causing him to hear instead that Juliet is dead. He obtains poison and decides to commit suicide by her side. Returning to Verona he encounters Paris at the entrance to the tomb. In the ensuing fight Paris is killed. Romeo then takes the poison, kisses the 'dead' Juliet and dies. Juliet wakes moments later, just as Frirar Laurence arrives on the scene in a vain attempt to avert tragedy. She stabs herself. The two families gather over the dead bodies and are reconciled after hearing the full story from the Friar.

SOURCES

Versions of this popular folklore tale exist in many languages but it is clear that Shakespeare closely followed an English translation (1562) by Arthur Brooke, *Romeus and Juliet*. It is possible that Shakespeare was at least aware of another English version by William Painter, 'Rhomeo and Julietta', included in the second volume of his popular collection of prose translations, *Palace of Pleasure*.

PART ONE: TEXT

1 INTRODUCTION

In 1662 *Romeo and Juliet* was performed in London in a version of the play adapted by James Howard which transformed the tragedy into a tragicomedy. According to one contemporary account, the two versions, Shakespeare's and Howard's, were 'Play'd Alternately, Tragical one Day, and Tragicomical another; for several Days together'. Such adaptations of various Elizabethan tragedies were popular after the Restoration but there is an interesting appropriateness in choosing this particular play, for the subject matter, much of the atmosphere of the first act and at least two of the play's most memorable characters, the Nurse and Mercutio, have long impressed critics as being more suited to comedy than tragedy. Shakespeare was of course always an innovator, even at the relatively early stage of his development as a playwright that marks the creation of *Romeo and Juliet*. The play was probably written between 1594 and 1596, at about the same time as *A Midsummer Night's Dream*, with which it has a number of features in common, although there have been arguments for an even earlier date. In writing *Romeo and Juliet*, Shakespeare took on a tale that at the very least a contemporary audience would have recognized as surprising raw material for tragedy. In fact one modern critic of the play has argued for more than surprise in the original audience's response. Harry Levin, in 'Form and Formality in *Romeo and Juliet*' (in *Shakespeare and the Revolution of the Times*, 1976, p. 108) says that audiences may well have been:

> surprised, and possibly shocked, at seeing lovers taken so seriously. Legend, it had been heretofore taken for granted, was the proper matter for serious drama; romance was the stuff of the comic stage ... [Shakespeare's] innovation might be described as transcending the usages of romantic comedy ...

This play's innovations have often made assessment – and performance – difficult. Modern directors have not gone quite so far as eighteenth-century adaptors in transforming the play into a tragicomedy but there have certainly been productions that stress the comic. In addition, the demands of the final act have proved particularly intractable. Textual critics have been similarly disturbed by what some have seen as the play's oddly broken-backed nature: two acts are written in a predominantly comic style, followed only after Mercutio's death by a last-half tragedy. Dr Johnson, among others, found the play's comic parts more interesting, but expressed disapproval over the preponderance of 'miserable conceits' – in other words, the play's frequent quips and puns. On the whole, modern critics are less disturbed by the perceived dramatic impropriety of linking grave matters with 'conceits', such as occurs most famously in Mercutio's pronouncement of his own death wound: 'ask for me tomorrow and you shall find me a grave man' (III i 98–9). However, the preponderance of such wit in the first half of what M. M. Mahood has described, in *Shakespeare's Wordplay* (1957), as 'one of Shakespeare's most punning plays', has contributed to the tendency to describe the play as a failed experiment in tragedy. G. Blakemore Evans, in his introduction to the New Cambridge edition (1984), describes critical reaction to it as ranging from 'simple adulation to measured disapproval' (p. 13). In performance Shakespeare's tendency to yoke together disparate emotions at key moments and the apparent shift in mood after Mercutio's death (which is often used as the appropriate point for an interval in modern productions) have led to responses that distinguish between first and second act, or between the play's youthful joy and its brooding tragedy. Only rarely has it been felt that a production has achieved full unity of effect without significant cuts to Shakespeare's text.

Parallel critical difficulties in assessing the success of the play centre on the question of the source of the tragedy. In the resulting debate Shakespeare is seen as an innovator, seeking to link the apparently inimical demands of two sorts of tragedy. On the one hand, the play may be interpreted within a framework implicit in the opening Chorus, in which the two lovers are described as 'star-cross'd' victims of a malign destiny, marked for tragedy at their birth, '[f]rom forth the fatal loins' of two feuding families. On the other hand, the tragedy is seen in broadly Aristotelian terms as originating in the characters of the two lovers. In such interpretations the words of Friar Laurence weigh heavily: '[w]isely and slow; they stumble that run fast' (II iii 90). Thus, from this perspective, the tragedy results from youthful impulse, evident in the lovers' reckless abandonment to youthful passion, which results in a series of disastrous choices. Inevitably these differing approaches have found differing theatrical expression. The tragedy of fate has been conveyed through the creation of a sense of brooding impending disaster, using the devices of lighting and design in particular to create an appropriate backdrop for the action. In what may be seen as a modern variation on the same approach, other directors have found ways of emphasizing the play's social context in order to suggest an inexorable pressure exerted upon the two lovers by Veronese society in general and the feuding families in particular. The abstract concept 'fate' is thereby given a local habitation and a name. On the other hand, theatrical expressions of the play as a tragedy of character have inevitably concentrated upon the lovers' temperaments, tending to give extra weight to their youth and giving full expression to the play's wilder extremes of emotion. In judging the play's success critics have all too often begun from one or other fixed position. Shakespeare's efforts are measured against a predetermined pattern that is supposed to fit all tragedy. The result, almost inevitably, is that Romeo does not quite fit the mould.

Although opinion is divided as to whether the play is a complete success, it is possible to discern a pattern which focuses attention on what seems to be one overriding aspect of Shakespeare's technique. This can be loosely described as a tendency to link opposites, so that the play's dominant idea seems to be akin to that which operates in oxymoron, a rhetorical device that dominates Romeo's opening scene. It is also closely linked to the paradoxes of Juliet's early premonition of her fate: '[m]y grave is like to be my wedding bed' (I v 134). Underlying a good deal of the poetic style is the tendency to take such contradictory ideas and then to attempt a resolution that does not deny the power of either term. In the language and the imagery of the play this often means that Shakespeare begins with the familiar terms of the Petrarchan sonnets of the second half of the sixteenth century. The influence exerted by Petrarch was largely against the native tradition of poets such as John Skelton, so that the style included a tendency to hyperbolic and highly decorative language. It also provided poets of the day with a ready-made stock of metaphors. In his own sonnet sequences Shakespeare showed himself to be both a master of Petrarchan conventions as well as a skilful parodist of its excesses. In *Romeo and Juliet* there are elements of both approaches and the effect, as the title to Anne Pasternak Slater's article on the subject puts it, is to make 'Petrarchanism come true in *Romeo and Juliet*' (printed in *Images of Shakespeare*, edited by Werner Habicht, 1988). In order to do this Shakespeare takes the paradoxes and hyperbole of Petrarchanism and then deploys them in the service of a tragedy which effectively enacts them on stage. The great experiment of *Romeo and Juliet* may therefore be described as an attempt to reshape the essentially private experience of the reader of a sonnet in the service of the public experience of theatrical tragedy.

2   LANGUAGE AND IMAGERY

The close affinity between much of the poetry of *Romeo and Juliet* and the highly wrought artifice of the Petrarchan sonnet can best be illustrated by a brief extract:

> Here's much to do with hate, but more with love.
> Why then, O brawling love, O loving hate,
> O anything of nothing first create!
> O heavy lightness, serious vanity,
> Misshapen chaos of well-seeming forms!
> Feather of lead, bright smoke, cold fire, sick health
> Still-waking sleep that is not what it is!
>
> (I i 175–81)

The style is hyperbolic, depending for its effect upon paradox and oxymoron, and employing a rather clumsy tautology: misshapen chaos. The play's close affinity with the sonnet itself is used to good effect at key moments. In its full fourteen-line form it appears at the opening of the first two acts and, most famously, in the first exchange between the two lovers but there are fragments of the form, often in six line chunks, evident throughout much of the first act in particular.

Through such bookish excesses as the example quoted above, Shakespeare conveys an initial impression of Romeo in which facile wit betrays the shallowness of his feelings in his professed love for Rosaline. At such moments Shakespeare seems simply to draw upon the ready-made supply of Petrarchan conceits as a foil to genuine emotions.

In the opening scenes Shakespeare also provides a bravura display of contrasting styles which serves to establish the background for the central love. The first of these is of course evident in the vulgar energy of the servants' prose exchanges which begin the play. Here the language is bawdy and clumsily witty with much play upon the loss of maidenheads. One effect of this comic style is that the audience is led to respond to the succeeding violence, and the arrival of old men crying out for their weapons, as essentially comic, rather than the initiation of a tragic sequence. The servants' bawdy also serves to prepare the way for Mercutio's infinitely more skilful variations on the same theme. The link between Mercutio and the servants ensures that from the outset we identify Mercutio with the 'common sense' of ordinary men.

Prince Escalus then makes the first of three entries. Structurally this establishes one of the play's important cyclical patterns, with the prince appearing at three key moments to restore order out of the chaos caused by the feuding families. Another pattern is the precisely delineated sequence of four days which emphasizes the lightning speed of the action and the extraordinary intensity of the central love affair. However, aside from such formal structuring, the play also displays a parallel tendency to patterning in the language. There is a habitual use of repetition within lines, such as these from early in the play:

> To wield **old** partisans, in hands as **old**,
> **Cank'red** with peace, to part your **cank'red** hate.
>
> (I i 94–5)

According to Harry Levin there are as many as 100 such lines in the play, primarily concentrated in the first two acts. In Levin's words such patterning can be described as 'the imposition of geometrical form upon the living data of formless consciousness', a technique normally associated with the comic (in 'Form and Formality in *Romeo and Juliet*', 1976, p. 113).

The address by Prince Escalus to the crowd establishes a contrasting voice to the style of the prose opening. Suddenly there is a shift to the formality of verse in which word play is employed to quite different effect. For example, a play on the word *temper* is used to underscore a rhetorical contrast between the dangers of brawling feuds and the appropriate behaviour of civilized men:

> You men, you beasts!
> That quench the fire of your pernicious rage
> With purple fountains issuing from your veins,
> On pain of torture from those bloody hands
> Throw your mistemper'd weapons to the ground . . . .
>
> (I i 81–5)

The urgings of the blood run counter to the activities of civilized man just as, symbolically, the civic fountains of Verona are turned to fountains of blood.

Yet another style characterizes the language of Montague. At this early stage in the play he describes his son's behaviour as a textbook case of melancholic love, employing the clichés of Petrarchan verse with no accompanying sense of irony. The style of his speeches may be linked to the similar language of Capulet's later description of Juliet's supposed grief at Tybalt's death. Both share a common source in the language of an outdated sonnet tradition that is clearly appropriate to such old men:

> *Montague*: Many a morning hath he there been seen,
>   With tears augmenting the fresh morning's dew,

> Adding to clouds more clouds with his deep sighs;
> But all so soon as the all-cheering sun
> Should in the farthest east begin to draw
> The shady curtains from Aurora's bed,
> Away from lights steals home my son
> And private in his chamber pens himself,
> Shuts up his windows, locks fair daylight out
> And makes himself an artificial night.
>
> (I i 129–37)

> *Capulet*: How now, a conduit, girl? What, still in tears?
> Evermore showering? In one little body
> Thou counterfeits a bark, a sea, a wind.
> For still thy eyes, which I may call the sea,
> Do ebb and flow with tears. The bark thy body is,
> Sailing in this salt flood, the winds thy sighs,
> Who raging with thy tears and they with them
> Without a sudden calm will overset
> Thy tempest-tossed body.
>
> (III v 129–37)

The formulaic imagery (linking tears and sighs with dew and clouds or describing the body as a ship sailing amid a sea of tears) underscores the extent to which the older generation is associated with an outmoded vocabulary and with rigid, formulaic patterns of thought. Indeed, as Anne Pasternak Slater suggests in 'Petrarchanism come true in *Romeo and Juliet*' (1988), Capulet's language in the example above is an imitation of an imitation, clumsily employing the phrases of a translation of one of Petrarch's sonnets by the mid-sixteenth-century poet Andrew Wyatt. Spotting such literary allusions may well have been one of the pleasures of Shakespeare's earliest audience but specific attribution of a source is not necessary to an appreciation of the point. Fortunately, through Mercutio's mockery Shakespeare conveniently supplies an implicit criticism of such out-of-fashion styles of an older generation. In Mercutio Shakespeare gives the audience the voice of cynical youth, knowingly mocking Romeo for being tied to 'the numbers that Petrarch flowed in'. Such numbers are evident in the stilted posturing of Romeo's description of love, which uses almost exactly the same metaphors (smoke, fumes, seas of tears) as those

found in the examples of the two fathers' speeches quoted
above:

> Love is a smoke made with the fume of sighs;
> Being purged, a fire sparkling in lovers' eyes;
> Being vexed, a sea nourished with lovers' tears.
>
> (I 1 190–2)

Romeo's early, bookish and artificial style is thereby linked to
the rigid thought processes of an older generation, preparing
the way for the change that is later effected by his love for
Juliet. At this stage in the play, however, it is indeed appropriate that Capulet's servant should turn to Romeo for help in
reading the guest list for the planned party. Throughout the
first act Romeo is the archetypal reader, one whose character
is almost entirely associated with a bookish wit.

   Having established several types of background music – the
earthy prose of the Veronese streets, the elevated formality of
authority and the dated imagery of old age – against which we
may form an initial impression of Romeo, Shakespeare then
introduces yet another voice. It is arguably the most innovative creation so far in the young playwright's career:

> Even or odd, of all days in the year,
> Come Lammas Eve at night shall she be fourteen.
> Susan and she – God rest all Christian souls –
> Were of an age. Well, Susan is with God;
> She was too good for me. But as I said,
> On Lammas Eve at night shall she be fourteen.
>
> (I iii 17–22)

The Nurse's speech was printed as prose in the two early
quartos printed during Shakespeare's lifetime, although most
modern editors have correctly recognized that it is a sort of
prosaic verse. In the most comprehensive analysis of the
Nurse's style, 'Juliet's Nurse: the uses of inconsequentiality'
(in *Shakespeare's Styles*, ed. Philip Edwards, 1980), Stanley
Wells speaks of Shakespeare's innovative uses of 'inconsequentiality' in establishing her distinctive voice and suggests
that the technique used here was fundamental to a number of
Shakespeare's greatest comic characterizations. The Nurse's
style is colloquial, digressive and apparently unstructured. All

of this helps to create an impression of earthy spontaneity that stands in marked contrast to the voices of the other members of the older generation in the play. This spontaneous energy, along with the hyperbolic fancy of Mercutio's wilder speeches, provide the play with two extremes which each help to shape our later impression of the distinctive style of the two lovers' exchanges.

Such then are some of the variety of voices which accumulate in the first acts of the play. Indeed, it should perhaps finally be noted that, amid all this abundance, there is one final 'voice' that can be said to operate as a sort of negative image, noticeable only by contrast to the others. Juliet is initially distinguished by how little she says. In her first appearance she is almost entirely passive, soliciting advice or simply listening to the Nurse's embarrassing garrulousness. There is a tendency among critics to search in all this for hints of the strength of will that she will later exhibit but the reader, and any actress who approaches the part, must primarily be struck by the fact that at this point in the play the text is remarkably open to interpretation in performance. For example, Juliet's interjection after one of the Nurse's longer digressions, 'stint thou too, I pray thee, Nurse, say I' (I iii 59), may be taken as a brief flash of the strong-willed character that emerges later in the play; it may equally be seen as a mixture of embarrassment and dutiful agreement with her mother's wishes. The age's approval of feminine docility is best illustrated through the words of Theseus in *A Midsummer Night's Dream*. Here another representative of mature male authority describes the ideal behaviour of girls of Juliet's age:

> Be advis'd, fair maid.
> To you your father should be as a god:
> One that compos'd your beauties, yea, and one
> To whom you are but as a form in wax
> By him imprinted, and within his power
> To leave the figure, or disfigure it.
>
> (I i 46–51)

It must be said that if there is more to Juliet than the docility advocated here, in the opening scenes there is little textual evidence to show for it.

Despite the variety of styles exhibited in the first few scenes, the result is more than simple confusion. Certain key image patterns, closely connected to the stock imagery of the sonnet traditions, begin to emerge. These develop from fundamental oppositions: light-dark, day-night, love-hate. From the outset, the traditionally strong associations between daylight and love and between dark and evil are used to define the conventional nature of Romeo's love for Rosaline. The fact that he chooses to make for himself 'an artificial night' by avoiding daylight is clearly seen to be unhealthy. Similarly Romeo's ludicrously ethereal definition of love as 'a smoke made with the fume of sighs' seems to be in irreconcilable conflict with the carnality of the servants. However, once these antitheses have been established in the opening scenes, their subsequent constant reiteration is used to subvert their traditional relationships, reaching a triumphant apotheosis in the brief exchange on the morning after their wedding. Here the traditional associations of night/day, light/dark are inverted. It is now suggested that the night is a friend, while daylight is an envious and malicious intruder, whose arrival Juliet clearly links with death: 'let day in, and let life out' (III v 41).

In addition to reversing the stock associations of Petrarchan imagery, Shakespeare often takes what had been traditionally used by poets as decorative flourishes and makes them central to the play's meaning. Nowhere is this more evident than in the stock association that linked death with a sexual lover. This standard image is given its most explicit statement in Capulet's lament over what he mistakenly believes to be Juliet's dead body, stolen from life on the day she was to marry Paris:

> O son, the night before thy wedding day
> Hath Death lain with thy wife. There she lies,
> Flower as she was, deflowered by him.
> Death is my son-in-law, Death is my heir,
> My daughter he hath wedded.
>
> (IV v 35–40)

Capulet's grief is no less sincere for being expressed in the familiar language of the sonneteers, which so often linked love and death. However, the pun on 'flower' and the operatic repetition of Death pose particular problems for an actor, particularly on the modern stage, before audiences who find such ritualized expressions of grief rather alien. In production, the moment is also richly ironic, not just because Juliet is alive but also because she is often seen lying on the bed which she has recently shared with her lover, Capulet's unknown son-in-law. He says far more than he can possibly realize, as the audience subsequently discover. Romeo's final address to his 'dead' lover in the Capulet family tomb will continue and develop these ironies, fixing permanently the image of Death as her lover. Indeed, as will be demonstrated in the close analysis of the play's final scenes, Shakespeare will re-deploy the imagery of defloration and of death-as-lover in such a way that they are greatly enriched.

3 THE LOVER'S COMPANIONS AND THE DRAMATIC CONTEXT

It is clear, therefore, that Shakespeare achieves a kind of harmony through variety in the play's language and imagery. The technique used is essentially comic, with many parallels to be found in the comedies of the same period. For example, *Love's Labour's Lost* also brings together a lavish variety of distinctive languages, from the courtly sonneteering of the Lords – which is not unlike Romeo's early style – to the blank incomprehension of Constable Dull. All are combined in a 'great feast of languages' that at the end of the play almost achieves the harmony of a comic resolution, only to be deferred by the intrusion of death. In *A Midsummer Night's Dream* Hippolyta provides the most familiar and succinct summary of the technique, by describing the various cries of Theseus's hunting hounds as 'musical discord ... sweet thunder'. However, such a technique is by no means the only one by which Shakespeare seeks to control the audience's responses to the story of the two lovers. As T. J. B. Spencer

describes it in his introduction to the New Penguin edition of
the play (1967):

> 'we observe the progressive isolation both of Juliet and of
> Romeo in their environments. Their love gradually separates
> them from their friends and families'.   (p. 28)

The linguistic aspect of this isolation is evident in the perceived lack of artifice in the style of the two lovers, a style
assessed by one of the play's most distinguished translators,
Boris Pasternak, thus: 'love has no need of euphony . . . truth,
not sound, dwells in its heart' (quoted by Levin in 'Form and
Formality', p. 109). Of course this apparent simple sincerity is
actually achieved by contrast with the even more elaborate
artifice of the styles seen in the first act of the play and,
therefore, is the result of skilfully concealed craft. One small
indication of this craft is the way that Shakespeare concen-
trates the use of rhymed verse in the first act, which is
abandoned almost entirely in the central acts, which contain
the lovers' exchanges, only to reappear after the lovers' deaths
in the re-established formality of the final reconciliations.

Aside from such purely stylistic devices, Shakespeare also
guides our emotional responses through the lovers' isolation
from their friends, and in this the figures of Mercutio and the
Nurse loom large. The two characters have a good deal in
common, each acting as both a foil and a companion/adviser
to one of the two lovers. In the Cambridge edition to the play
G. Blakemore Evans has suggested that it is their 'easy
opportunism' that ultimately contrasts most starkly with the
lovers' 'complete commitment to an ideal' (p. 23).

In creating the Nurse, Shakespeare accepted the broad
outlines of his source, Arthur Brooke's verse romance, *Romeus
and Juliet*. However, whereas Brooke is unambiguous about
the Nurse's age, referring to her as 'olde' and 'ancient',
Shakespeare is far less clear. In his play she is both 'auncient
damnation' and yet young enough to have suckled Juliet.
Naturally this creates significant difficulties on the stage –
difficulties which may be less obvious from reading the play,
since a director does not have the luxury of such ambiguity; a
decision must be made about who is to play the role.
Traditional representations, including most famously Edith

Evans, have tended to emphasize her age, while more recent
directors have explored other possibilities. It seems probable
that Shakespeare intended to place particular emphasis upon
the Nurse's old age, particularly if we bear in mind that by
doing so he placed contrasting emphasis upon Juliet's extreme
youth. Here again Shakespeare alters his source: Brooke
makes Juliet sixteen while in the play she is not yet fourteen.
The Nurse's constant rambling stories about the past may be
linked with a number of such references running throughout
the play, such as Capulet's own memories of his youth:

> I have seen the day
> That I have worn a visor and could tell
> A whispering tale in a fair lady's ear,
> Such as would please. 'Tis gone, 'tis gone, 'tis gone!
>
> (I v 22–6)

All of the older generation contribute to this accumulating
sense of the past, but it is the Nurse above all who provides the
play's sense of a wider temporal context that extends beyond
the brief four days of the play's action. Through her we are
made aware, as T. J. B. Spencer says, of a world in which
'people have grown old, had their frolics and miseries over
many years' (p. 34). The contrast between an extended past
and the terrible brevity of the play's action affects us in several
different ways. Most profoundly of course the references evoke
a past which is ostensibly the world of 'wisely and slow',
where people do not 'stumble' from haste. It is such wisdom
that is shown to be so decidedly lacking in the last few scenes
of the play, particularly in the attempts by both the Nurse and
Friar Laurence to comfort and guide their youthful charges.
The lightning flash of the central love affair stands out against
the background of such worldly wisdom and is valued all the
more as a result of the contrast. Of course, the Nurse can
hardly be described as mere background. Above all else she is
a beloved friend and confidante. Juliet's dependence upon this
friendship is strengthened by the absence of any apparent
strong bonds with her mother and her final isolation is
heightened by the fact that she feels herself to have been
betrayed by her only friend.

It is tempting to take Juliet at her word when she disavows

her lifelong friendship for the Nurse and proclaims her to be 'a most wicked fiend'. However, Shakespeare is at some pains to indicate both the depth of the Nurse's affection and the difficulties of her social position. Simon Trussler, writing in the playtext/programme that accompanied the 1988 Royal Shakespeare Company production of the play, is surely correct to defend her for her counsel of 'pragmatic bigamy' on the grounds that it constitutes 'a matter of pure self-preservation' by a woman whose position in the family is entirely dependent upon patronage. She could hardly expect thanks for her involvement in Juliet's marriage to an exiled enemy of the family but, as a faithful retainer, she might well be treated well by a wealthy man such as Paris. Seen from this point of view there is a sensible consistency of attitude here; we may well recognize that she is 'right' to do what she does, even as her calm betrayal of Romeo's love provokes an emotional revulsion. Indeed her behaviour can be understood as an expression of deep concern for a young child's welfare. Brenda Bruce, who played the role in a 1984 production, says this of the moment:

> Anything is better than family rejection, starvation. There would be nothing for a girl, alone in the world – only begging on the streets.
>
> (Quoted in *Players of Shakespeare 2*, 1988 p. 100)

This appeal to self-preservation is of course also the basis for Friar Laurence's later behaviour: 'I dare no longer stay' (v iii 159). Therefore, for an audience to share Juliet's revulsion with the Nurse for her actions at this point of the play would seem to require that we share a perspective that runs counter to the traditional mature wisdom exhibited by both the Nurse and Friar Laurence. Part of the tragic momentum that the play develops in the final two acts results precisely from the fact that Shakespeare is at such pains to make the Nurse's dismissal by Juliet so painfully affecting but utterly inevitable. In short, it requires that we give witness to the validity of Romeo's early oxymoron, 'loving hate'.

The sense of inevitability which dominates much of the later action in the play has often been judged against the frame of reference provided by the play's opening sonnet, with

its emphasis upon malign fate. Critical debates on this point
have tended to depend upon a pre-determined pattern to
which tragedy is expected to comply, yet the play as a
theatrical experience rarely fits the pattern. The play depends
upon a crucial paradox that twins destiny and choice. Its
success also depends upon our sympathy with the voices of
wisdom, even as we acknowledge the demands of a love that
transcends such wisdom. We are similarly asked to acknowledge the appeal of Mercutio's reductive view of love-as-sex,
even as we later recognize that such a view has little place
within the play's more comprehensive representation of romantic love.

What links Mercutio with the Nurse is their essentially
mechanistic view of life. Their advice ultimately matches
closely Benvolio's well-meaning suggestion to Romeo at the
start of the play:

> Tut man, one fire burns out another's burning,
> One pain is lessen'd by another's anguish.
>
> (I ii 45–6)

Of course, as the Nurse sees it, it is even better if the pain of
Juliet's loss of Romeo can be 'burned out' by the handsome
County Paris. We may spot much the same attitude, albeit
under far more extreme pressures, in Friar Laurence's suggestion that Juliet can be disposed of in a convent once Romeo is
dead. For Mercutio the case is more complicated, but the fatal
challenge to Tybalt may perhaps best be seen as a desperate
throw to displace Romeo's supposed affection for Rosaline.
The previous scene had linked Rosaline and Tybalt, with
Romeo apparently the focus of attention:

> *Mercutio:* Why, that same pale hard-hearted wench, that
> Rosaline,
> Torments him so that he will sure run mad.
> *Benvolio:* Tybalt, the kinsman to old Capulet,
> Hath sent a letter to his father's house . . .
>
> (II iv 4–7)

The thoughts of a recent actor of the part suggest a curious
linkage, which has too often been clumsily interpreted in

terms of a homosexual rivalry, between the way that Mercutio
seems marginalized by this exchange and his subsequent
decision to take Tybalt's challenge upon himself. Roger
Allam, who played Mercutio in a production by the Royal
Shakespeare Company in 1983/4, describes the scene in the
following terms:

> Mercutio is very quickly informed by Benvolio that Romeo has
> not been home all night and that, by letter, Tybalt has
> challenged Romeo to a duel. For Mercutio these two facts are
> immediately connected .... The thought begins to form in
> Mercutio's mind that he could fight Tybalt in Romeo's stead.
> Fight him, beat him, and, as it were, psychically win back
> Romeo by saving him physically.
>
> (*Players of Shakespeare 2*, 1988, p. 116)

Displace one threat by challenging another seems to be the
subtext: 'burn out' one fire with another. Of course, the tragic
irony is that Mercutio is fighting a foe that he does not know,
just as earlier he and Benvolio had 'jested at scars that never
felt a wound'. Shakespeare has already ensured that the issue
is pre-judged, not through the play's references to fate, but
through Mercutio's display of outlandish fantasy, in the Queen
Mab speech. If Mercutio's perspective depends entirely upon
the reduction of the spiritual element in favour of the purely
physical, then he is condemned out of his own mouth. His
Queen Mab speech constitutes a tacit admission that his
exclusive appeal to the senses is inadequate and prepares the
ground for the play's final scene, where transcendant love is
seen to triumph. However, the play does not simply present
the issue as one of competing views of love and sex, for the
transcendence of the final act is not achieved by rejecting the
physical but through a consummation with it. It is this that
underlies both Romeo's final pun (Thus with a kiss I die) and
the erotic imagery of Juliet's final words:

> Oh happy dagger.
> This is thy sheath. There rust, and let me die.
> (v iii 169–70)

It is in the final controversial scene that Shakespeare most
clearly attempts to achieve the culmination of what I have

already described as a technique based on oxymoron and upon the paradoxical realization of stock Petrarchan imagery. It is a scene that ventures and achieves a great deal, a triumphant but ultimately flawed experiment, and as such it deserves careful consideration.

4 AMOROUS DEATH: ACT V, SCENE III

The division of any of Shakespeare's plays into acts and scenes often misleads readers into neglecting the seamless flow and pacing that are possible on a stage uncluttered by excessive scenery. In this particular instance we must bear in mind that on the sort of stage that is commonly conjectured for Elizabethan productions of the play Juliet's mock death at the end of Act IV would have led in an unbroken sequence to the events of Act V. On a functional level the comic exchanges by the musicians that end Act IV would have occupied the foreground, while Juliet's bed was hidden behind a curtain in the upstage alcove that was probably part of the standard Elizabethan stage design. Romeo's entrance at the beginning of the next act would then have taken place directly in front of the curtained alcove that contained Juliet's drugged body; the same space would be in turn transformed into the tomb for the final scene. Given appropriate staging the text therefore is richly ironic, as it fuses the tragi-comic grief over Juliet's 'dead' body with the increasingly tragic claustrophobia of the final scenes. Capulet's description perfectly captures the confusion of moods:

> All things that we ordained festival
> Turn from their office to black funeral:
> Our instruments to melancholy bells,
> Our wedding cheer to a sad burial feast;
> Our solemn hymns to sullen dirges change,
> Our bridal flowers serve for a buried corse;
> And all things change them to the contrary.
>
> (IV v 84–90)

Shakespeare would later return to the same paradoxes in *Hamlet* for the grotesque image of the 'funeral baked meats' that Hamlet says are used to coldly furnish his mother's wedding feast. In *Romeo and Juliet* this jumble of contradictory emotions and images precedes a final-act resolution that extends the range of paradoxes yet further.

At the beginning of Act v Romeo speaks with something of the hyperbolic imagination that he has exhibited in earlier scenes: 'how sweet is love itself possessed,/When but love's shadows are so rich in joy!' However, there is a greater sense of control over the rhetoric (combined with the fact that his imagination is now firmly grounded in experience) and there is an underlying sense of foreboding in his dream of death, which anticipates the final scene in the tomb. However, it is his response to Balthasar's news that most clearly marks a significant change of character. As he is later to do, to much the same effect, in *Hamlet*, Shakespeare chooses to allow a passage of time, albeit in this case brief, and an absence from the scene, for the change in character to occur. One need only recall Romeo's recent behaviour in the face of adversity, when he is quite unmanned with grief, to recognize the extent of the alteration. Told of his banishment by Friar Laurence, Romeo had thrown himself to the floor in an ecstasy of self-pity which displayed a complete disregard for Juliet's danger:

> Hadst thou no poison mixed, no sharp-ground knife,
> No sudden mean of death, though ne'er so mean,
> But 'banished' to kill me – 'banished'?
> O Friar, the damned use that word in hell.
>
> (III iii 45–8)

Now, his reaction to the news of Juliet's death displays a quiet resolution that is quite new: 'Is it e'en so? Then I defy you, stars!' (v i 24). The contrast is made yet more striking by his calm control over the apothecary, who is described in terms that parody the first appearance of the Friar:

> I do remember an apothecary –
> And hereabouts 'a dwells – which late I noted
> In tatter'd weeds, with overwhelming brows,
> Culling of simples.   (v i 37–40)

It is tempting to imagine a doubling of the roles of Friar Laurence and the Apothecary. This is just about feasible and would require no more than a quick change of robe but, as Jill Levenson has observed in her discussion of the early staging of the play in *'Romeo and Juliet': Shakespeare in Performance* (1987), such doubling would be unlikely, if only for the fact that the Friar is already one of the play's largest roles. Nevertheless, Romeo's dependence upon such an ally indicates this desperate resolve and any parallel that the audience may sense between Friar Laurence and the Apothecary would certainly serve to heighten the already strong sense of the distance that Romeo has travelled since the start of the play. Paradoxically, it is precisely Romeo's greater maturity and resolve that precipitates the tragedy, since from this point on the play depends absolutely upon the precise timing with which events occur. This is only one of the ways in which the insistently repeated imagery of lightning speed is given theatrical expression. As Caroline Spurgeon, in *Shakespeare's Imagery and What It Tells Us* (1935), a pioneering examination of the play's iterative imagery, claimed:

> There can be no question, I think that Shakespeare saw the story, in its swift and tragic beauty, as an almost blinding flash of light, suddenly ignited, and as swiftly quenched.   (p. 127)

Similarly, the brief appearance by the Friar in V ii serves not only to provide the necessary information about the delayed message, but to heighten our sense of the reckless speed of Romeo's actions. This same haste and desperate resolve first leads to Paris's death, as he is innocently swept up in events.

The play's early depiction of Paris as Romeo's rival in love is almost entirely unsympathetic. For example, he is seen to be insensitive to Juliet's true feelings when he encounters her in Friar Laurence's cell. Earlier, in the first act, he had been described by Lady Capulet, with no hint of irony on her part, in terms that she takes to be flattering but which actually tell against him. He is 'a man of wax', a 'book of love'; terms that associate him with Romeo's early childish behaviour but with none of Romeo's redeeming wit. At the start of the final act Shakespeare reintroduces the character, primarily as a foil to Romeo. However, in a quite characteristic touch and without any sacrifice of consistency, Shakespeare provides for the minor character a part in the play's widening tragic pattern.

Paris is every bit the lover of the sonnets, performing quite conventional acts of grief, and the language at this point of the play reverts to the formality of rhyme that had dominated the first act:

> Sweet flower, with flowers thy bridal bed I strew.
> O woe, thy canopy is dust and stones
> Which with sweet water nightly I will dew,
> Or wanting that, with tears distill'd by moans.
> The obsequies that I for thee will keep
> Nightly shall be to strew thy grave and weep.
>
> (v iii 12–17)

The scene anticipates the rituals that will be required in *Much Ado About Nothing* round the supposed grave of Hero; in both cases the formality contrasts with the spontaneity exhibited by the dominant (although of course in terms of the plot in *Much Ado* Benedick and Beatrice are technically subordinate) pair of lovers, Benedick and Beatrice. In neither play is this formality meant to suggest a lack of sincerity, merely that such love pales beside the other couples' less rigid expressions of love. Paris is swept up in events, killed in a fight that Romeo wants to avoid and then dragged into the tomb to take a place, albeit a peripheral one, in the final tableau. Shakespeare indicates the extent to which Romeo has changed during the four short days of the play by emphasizing Paris's youth. Although Romeo can be little older in years, he calls Paris 'gentle youth . . . youth . . . boy . . . slaughter'd youth' and, with unaffected simplicity, acknowledges Paris's right to a place in the tragic pattern of 'sour misfortune's book'.

The sequence of events leading up to the twin suicides that mark the climax of the play therefore involves a careful preparation of audience sympathies. All of this is often discarded in performance. Although Shakespeare does not attempt to universalize the tragedy after the fashion later used in the great tragedies of state, such as *King Lear* or *Macbeth*, there is a clear attempt in the last act to expand the focus by implicating everyone present on stage in the final tableau. One additional consequence of such scenes is that the sense of

the central characters' culpable rashness is diminished, as
both Paris and Friar Laurence are also seen to be caught up
by the rush of events.

Romeo's death fulfils his earlier promise that he would lie
with Juliet that night, thereby enacting on stage the Petrarchan conceit which links love and death. Brian Gibbons, in his
introduction to the Arden edition of the play, provides a
number of appropriate parallels in the poetry of Shakespeare's contemporaries, such as this from Samuel Daniel's
'Rosamund':

> Ah how me thinks I see death dallying seekes,
> To entertaine it self in loues sweet place

The moment brings into perfect focus many of the play's
recurrent images, most notably those related to light and
dark. To some extent limited by the facilities of his own stage,
Shakespeare must use the repeated references by Romeo and
Paris to establish the fact that the scene takes place in the light
of a solitary torch. However, as Anne Pasternak Slater
reminds us, the presence of torches has been an important
theatrical counterpart to the imagery throughout the play,
from the first meeting of the two lovers, lit by torchbearers
('Petrarchanism come true in *Romeo and Juliet*', p. 142).
Today a director may well take advantage of modern lighting
to underscore Romeo's ecstatic description of Juliet:

> For here lies Juliet, and her beauty makes
> This vault a feasting presence, full of light.
>   (v iii 85–6)

However, on the Elizabethan stage the effect is almost entirely
verbal rather than visual, even if the actors carry the implied
stage props of torches and lanterns. The scene fuses all the
Petrarchan conceits that had characterized Romeo's earlier
risible efforts as a poet manqué. It is, as Brian Gibbons has
suggested, a triumphant vindication of the supposedly tired
clichés of the sonnet tradition:

> So, at last, the rote-learned sonneteering paradoxes are lived
> out actually; in the intensity of the tragic climax fire and ice are

simultaneously felt, drugs at once quick and deadly. To kiss is
to die in earnest: the living moment and the poem coincide.

(p. 52)

Juliet's own suicide is treated much more summarily.
Having reached one emotional climax, Shakespeare sur-
rounds the second with the threat of sudden interruption so
that Friar Laurence's well-intentioned attempts to interfere
are made to look quite clearly out of touch. The Friar's
thoughts are of the future and his offer to 'dispose' of Juliet
among a sisterhood of nuns is characteristically sensible, yet
even in this the advocate of temperate slowness is overtaken
by circumstance. He shows a somewhat surprising concern at
the thought of punishment by a temporal ruler; Shakespeare
seems to imply that for all the Friar's deliberations his actions
are as hasty as those he sought to advise and, whatever the
merits of his council in general, there is little doubt that the
dramatic context in this case tells strongly against him.

The remainder of the play falls into three segments: the
entrance of the Prince with the citizenry of Verona, Friar
Laurence's recapitulation and the final tableau of reconciliation. All three have suffered from the director's cuts in
productions stretching back through the nineteenth century.
The extent to which the audience's final impression of the
play, once the central lovers have been satisfactorily killed off,
can be affected by the whims of the director may most clearly
be seen in the following account by John Harrison, who
played Benvolio and Chorus in Peter Brook's production of
1947:

> [Brook] left a great deal to chance inspiration at the dress
> rehearsal. It was not until then, for example, if memory serves
> me right, that he decided to cut the reconciliation of the houses
> (the only point to the play, apart from the poetry which he'd
> strewn on the floor) and awarded the Prince of Verona's final
> speech to me as Chorus.
> (Printed in J. C. Trewin's *Peter Brook – A Biography*, 1971, p. 35)

The attitude toward the text displayed here is not new.
Brook's treatment sentimentalized the ending, much as David
Garrick had done for his own productions in 1748 by rewriting

the ending in order to include the following highly affecting
exchange between the two lovers:

> *Romeo:* ... Eyes look your last;
>   Arms take your last embrace; and lips do you
>   The doors of breath seal with a righteous kiss.
>   Soft! soft! She breathes and stirs!
>   *Juliet wakes.*
> *Juliet:* Where am I? Defend me, powers!
> *Romeo:* She speaks, she lives! And we shall be blessed!
> (In David Garrick's *Plays*, eds H. Pedicord and F. Bergman,
> 1981)

The common element in both versions is a refusal to confront
the play's final public rituals.

As I have already observed, the entrance of the Prince
completes the play's carefully established rhythm of violence
suspended by the voice of authority. This, along with the
Friar's summary of the events of the preceding few days, plays
an important part in the play's representation of authority as
the focus for a collective acknowledgement of responsibility
and compassion. As John Russell Brown notes in 'S. Franco
Zeffirelli's *Romeo and Juliet*', in *Shakespeare Survey 14* (1962),
the theme of 'responsibility learnt in adversity' recurs in a
number of Shakespeare's works, including *Richard II, Henry V,
King Lear, Pericles, Cymbeline, The Winter's Tale* and *The
Tempest* (p. 153). In *Romeo and Juliet* the Prince specifically
accepts his involvement in the guilt as well as the suffering:

> Capulet, Montague,
> See what a scourge is laid upon your hate,
> That heaven finds means to kill your joys with love;
> And I, for winking at your discords too,
> Have lost a brace of kinsmen. All are punish'd.
>   (v iii 290–4)

Although in general Shakespeare followed his source material
quite closely, the Prince's acceptance of guilt is Shakespeare's
own addition, suggesting that it is something to which he
attaches particular weight. There is nothing facile or easily
won about the reconciliation between the two families. The
promise to construct a golden monument in the lover's memory

should not be seen as the shallow opportunism of two old men who cannot feel deeply enough to grieve. The time and care with which Shakespeare arranges for each party to be brought centre stage before the assembled citizenry to be questioned, and the final understated hand-clasp of reconciliation between the two old men, all provide an appropriate conclusion to a tragedy that has consistently acknowledged the tension between the public demands of birth and blood and the private impulses of the heart.

5 CONCLUSION: WORD AND IMAGE

The history of *Romeo and Juliet*, both in performance and as a text for critical scrutiny, has inevitably been dominated by the eponymous heroes. However, this has almost certainly had some serious consequences which may well have distorted our perception of the play. To some extent the difficulties faced by modern audiences may be attributed to the inevitable changes in theatrical taste which affect any of Shakespeare's plays. For example, in his New Penguin edition of the play, T. J. B. Spencer suggests two such serious consequences: first, our difficulty in understanding some of Mercutio's complex puns tends to 'soften' his impact in modern performance; moreover, the Friar's moralizing is 'rendered weaker than Shakespeare's text authorizes' (p. 8). In fact it is probably true that much of what has often been taken as simply the background to the lovers has been undervalued, so that we are tempted to concentrate our attention upon questions centred upon the lovers' rashness while ignoring the importance of the self-perpetuation of violence as well as the lovers' role in its final exorcism. Simon Trussler reminds us that the modern tendency to read the play through the filter of a pre-determined definition of tragedy which focuses exclusively upon the lovers' flaws can result in disastrous interpretations:

> What a grievous symptom of the working assumptions of our
> society that the one character in the play who achieves, for all

its brevity, a happy and mutually fulfilled sexual relationship, the one character [Romeo] who, however disastrous the consequences, actually tries to step between violent antagonists, should be regarded as immoderate! (Programme/Playtext to 1988 RSC production)

The expression of shock here is slightly disingenuous, as the play makes abundantly clear that it is always the 'wise, slow' voices of reason who will pass such judgement and Shakespeare certainly retains traces of Arthur Brooke's disapprobative attitude toward the 'drunken gossips and superstitious friars' who surround the lovers. However, it is only by giving full weight to the play's so-called background that the full depth of the tragedy may be measured, and we may recognize, as the final exchanges force us to do, that the play's most fundamental lack of moderation lies not with the lovers but with their elders. Such an awareness of the significance of the social context of the play is clearly vital. On occasion, particularly in production, these background issues are given excessive emphasis, as may be seen from this comment by Michael Bogdanov, the director of a production discussed in Part Two:

At the end of *Romeo and Juliet* there is a little scene between the Apothecary and Romeo, in which Romeo says that gold is the real poison in people's souls. Again, at the end of that play we see the Capulets and the Montagues vying with each other to see who can erect the biggest gold statue to the memory of their offspring. (Quoted in *The Shakespeare Myth*, ed. Graham Holderness, 1988, p. 94)

There can be little doubt that the society depicted in the play is flawed, and that the older generation are guilty of insensitivity to their children as well as being tainted by their longstanding feud, but Bogdanov is surely misguided to place these issues in the foreground and to conclude, as he goes on to do, that the tragedy is entirely a question of:

greed and avarice on the part of Capulet insisting that his daughter marries someone close to the seat of power: Escalus's nephew Paris.

The text provides scant support for such a view, and Capulet is quite clearly seen to be concerned about his daughter's wishes and to have her happiness at the centre of his actions. He is misguided, and rather autocratic, but his social aspirations, particularly when seen in the context of Elizabethan marriage arrangements, do not constitute 'the main cancer at the heart of a society' as Bogdanov wishes to claim. Developing the audience's awareness of the social and cultural pressures upon the central lovers clearly demands a careful balancing act.

However, there are additional difficulties that arise from Shakespeare's experimental approach to the creation of tragedy, particularly with regard to his attempt to give dramatic expression to the language and techniques of the sonnet. Peter Brook, looking back after twenty years upon his 1947 production, described his approach in terms that suggest the modern director's difficulties in staging a play that is so completely dominated by essentially private verbal effects:

> Scenery is irresistibly fascinating. For me the theatre always begins with an image. If I find the image through the design, I know how to continue with the production.... Yet over the years I have worked always against the scenery – in reaction away from scenery. When Rolf Gerard [the designer] and I did *Romeo and Juliet* at Stratford we began throwing out our own scenery at the dress rehearsal. Gradually we came down to an empty orange arena, a few sticks – and the wings were full of elaborate and expensive discarded units. We were very proud of ourselves, but the management was furious.... Nothing is so beautiful as a bare stage: yet its loneliness and its openness is often too strong a statement and it must be enclosed.
>
> (Quoted in J. C. Trewin's biography, p. 32–3)

In such a statement we may witness the honest struggle by one gifted director to come to terms with the demands generated by Shakespeare's text. It is a struggle that certainly would not have troubled nineteenth-century directors of the play. A brief extract from a description of Henry Irving's 1882 Lyceum production suggests just how little such concerns weighed upon the mind of one of the century's most admired actor-managers. After listing the scenic beauties of 'the market place of Verona', into which Romeo enters 'by the sloping bridge at the back', . . . and of the 'loggia of Capulet's house', and of the 'hall in Capulet's house – one of the richest and most brilliant scenes that has been witnessed' the description by Austin Brereton, in an annual publication called *Dramatic Notes*, concludes rather ecstatically:

> One might have thought that scenic art could go no further, but the street in Mantua, in the fifth act, revealed a picture of great beauty; and the tomb scene, with its entrance down several flights of steps, leading from the roof, was a marvel of scenic success, and the tableau at the conclusion of the play brought to a close one of the grandest spectacular representations of a Shakespearian play that has ever been presented.
> (Quoted in C. D. Odell, *Shakespeare from Betterton to Irving*, 1966, Vol 2, p. 427)

Peter Brook's struggles to resist the temptations of scenery take us a long way from such excesses, yet we do well to bear in mind that this is not a struggle that would have occurred in the earliest productions on the almost bare stage of Shakespeare's theatre. In general, of course, much the same could be said of any of Shakespeare's plays, with the possible exception of the later Romances, where scenic effects seem to begin to take on greater significance. There is, however, an important sense in which *Romeo and Juliet* places unique emphasis upon certain linguistic effects. Nicholas Brooke, in *Shakespeare's Early Tragedies* (1968), indicates the primary area of difficulty when he says that 'in fact the play can partly be seen as a dramatic exploration of the world of the love sonnet'. This, however, is an essentially private world developed through a verse form of sophisticated artifice. The dual challenge created by this mixture is perfectly illustrated by the famous sonnet exchanged by the two lovers at their first meeting. The event is both public and utterly circumscribed from the outside world. Any production of the play must simultaneously suggest the noise and bustle of a lively party in a great household and the complete isolation of instant recognition and shared thought needed to make the sonnet's artifice seem appropriate. Richard David provides an astute description of the director's challenge in *Shakespeare in the Theatre*, contrasting the approach taken by some directors,

who seek completely to isolate the two lovers in a charmed
world away from the party, with 'Shakespeare's design',
which is:

> more effectively preserved if that world, with which the lovers
> are to war, remains visually present too, so that the lovers' first
> meeting takes place not in absolute isolation but in a private
> enclave, a secret momentary bubble. . . . The sonnet-form styl-
> ises the moment and sets it on a pedestal; but if the lovers are
> physically, as well as verbally, isolated the artificiality becomes
> too great.   (p. 29)

The primary ground upon which the play's meaning is
worked out is that of the artifice of the play's constantly
contradictory language. The greatest difficulty facing the
director of the play on the modern stage lies in the need to find
a medium which will allow a text that is centred on such
linguistic devices as the oxymoron to take shape on a stage
that has become much more clearly dominated by the image.
Increasingly, this has caused directors to move in a direction
whose logical end point may well be the cinema rather than
the theatre. A comment made by Roy Walker in 'In Fair
Verona' (in C. W. Eckert, ed., *Focus on Shakespearean Films*,
1972) has suggested that the direction for Shakespearian
production in general 'is to create a new synthesis of speech
and spectacle'. It is perhaps no surprise that arguably the
most successful 'production' of *Romeo and Juliet* has been
Franco Zeffirelli's film version, which extended the experimental approach to the play taken in his previous Old Vic
stage production of 1961. Both on stage and on the screen,
Zeffirelli's approach had essentially been to translate the
language of the text by using the grammar of film. However,
the process involved a significant transformation of the original and, as will be seen in Part Two, Zeffirelli certainly
displayed little interest in maintaining the text. Instead,
Zeffirelli's approach can best be described as one of substitu-
tion, in which he replaces the density of language with an
equivalent density of image. After all, in shaping the film
version Zeffirelli cut more than half of the text, with very little
loss in the overall length of the final product.
   It is worth ending an assessment of this relatively early and

flawed tragedy with an extract from Dr Johnson's sound appraisal of Shakespearian drama in general:

> Shakespeare's plays are not in the rigorous and critical sense either tragedies or comedies, but compositions of a distinct kind; exhibiting the real state of sublunary nature, which partakes of good and evil, joy and sorrow, mingled with endless variety of proportion and innumerable modes of combinations. . . .
> (Quoted from *Dr Johnson on Shakespeare*, ed. W. K. Wimsatt, Penguin, 1960, p. 62)

It may well be that at this point in his career Shakespeare is not able to achieve the full synthesis of good and evil, joy and sorrow, but in *Romeo and Juliet* we may certainly see the outlines of the distinctive method of the later plays. It seems that at this point in his career Shakespeare is perfectly capable of writing much affecting poetry and a good deal of highly successful stagecraft but it may be argued that the two are not always entirely successfully blended. However, if the play has its undoubted flaws they arise from the extent of the challenge he set himself in trying to link such disparate moods within a plot that owes so much to comedy and while using a technique that draws so much from the sonnet tradition. We may be sure that the Elizabethans were concerned with the individuality of the experiment, not with questions about the predetermined category of tragedy into which the play should be placed.

PART TWO: PERFORMANCE

6 INTRODUCTION

Romeo and Juliet is a perennial favourite on the stage. In the twentieth century it is only eclipsed by *Hamlet* for the frequency of major professional productions. As with all of Shakespeare's plays the information regarding the first productions is sketchy, although there is some evidence to suggest that the stage directions printed in the quarto editions of 1597 and 1599 give some bare information on early staging. Such information is inevitably undetailed, even random, but as recent editors of the play have noted, some light is thrown by it on occasional scenes. For example, references are made to such things as whispering, to entries above (on the balcony) and to some of the movable props that would have been used to create the minimal sense of specific locality which was all that Shakespeare's audience required. The text itself is of course rich in reference to certain key features of what may be called the stage of the imagination. Although *Romeo and Juliet* is a young man's play, Shakespeare has already learned to take advantage of the flexibility of the relatively bare Elizabethan stage, particularly in the heightened imaginative involvement that it demands and in the opportunities for dramatically effective juxtapositions of scenes. For example, Paris's reference at the opening of v iii, to strewing Juliet's bridal bed with flowers is all the more affecting for being literally true. The undercurrent of eroticism that accompanies his final speech gains dramatic impact for much the same reasons.

Pepys recorded his dislike of a performance of the play in 1662 as being 'the first time it was ever acted', presumably since the original performances. The fact that the play was subsequently adapted as a tragi-comedy perhaps indicates that seventeenth-century audiences found the comedy of the

original version as difficult to accommodate as have modern
directors. However, it is certainly the case that for nearly 200
years there were virtually no productions that retained the
original text, even heavily cut. The emphasis throughout the
eighteenth and nineteenth centuries was primarily upon ten-
der and affecting passions which would wrench the heart of
the audience, often ending, as with Garrick's adaptation, with
a tearful reunion between the two lovers before their deaths.
Modern directors have been influenced by this tradition, even
as they move steadily away from it. It must also be admitted
that modern directors have often felt little compunction about
'improving' the text, particularly when dealing with the play's
final scene. Although it is rare for a modern director to add
lines, quite a number have been at least as ruthless as their
theatrical forebears about the segment of the play that follows
the lovers' deaths. Garrick cut perhaps half of the last 150
lines; in 3 of the play's most significant post-war directors,
Peter Brook (1947), Franco Zeffirelli (1961) and Michael
Bogdanov (1986), have each dispensed with almost all of the
final lines. Indeed, given the immense popularity of Franco
Zeffirelli's film version of the play, it follows that most modern
audiences are primarily familiar with the final scene in a
cut-down version.

Despite such cuts the play has rarely matched the Chorus's
promise of a 'two hours traffic'. Often the delay has been
caused by an insistence upon elaborate scenic effects such as
Henry Irving's division of the final scene in order to use two
lavish sets. As a result of such elaborations, the play is rarely
less than three hours long and often runs closer to four hours,
thereby significantly altering the audience's impression of the
tragedy's rapid, unstoppable momentum. As Brian Gibbons
has observed, in the introduction to the Arden edition, in this
play 'speed is the medium of fate' and a director must give this
the appropriate theatrical expression.

Modern productions have often foundered over two related
difficulties: the challenge of the play's mixture of comedy and
tragedy and the tendency for a production to fall into two
ill-matched halves. The curious mixture of material, which is
in many respects traditionally most suited to comic treatment,
has led to difficulties in the representation of ancillary charac-

ters, especially the Nurse and Mercutio. This in turn seems
linked to an often-noted disparity between the relative success
of the two halves of the play. Roughly speaking the turning
point seems to come with the deaths of Mercutio and Tybalt.
Some productions have succeeded in capturing the youthful
optimism, bustling activity and bawdy comedy of the first
half; others have managed to convey a mood of impending
doom that is felt to be appropriate to the final half. Few have
achieved the balanced mingling of these apparently immisible
moods that would allow an 'ideal' production. Both Brook's
1947 production and Zeffirelli's 1961 stage version, at the Old
Vic, were notably successful in conveying the bustle of a
crowded Italian city and youthful energy of the two lovers;
however, the fact that both directors had to resort to radical
cutting of the last act is symptomatic of their struggles to
manage the second half of the play. Productions have occasionally been dominated by Mercutio or the Nurse, or both, a sure
sign that a director has fallen prey to the temptation to allow
these essentially comic characters to run out of control. For
instance, Dame Edith Evans dominated Peter Hall's 1961
production in a performance that has justly been regarded a
classic but the production may well have suffered as a result.

Hall's production also illustrated perhaps the greatest
single difficulty faced by any director of the play: casting
precisely the right central characters. Two things are needed
for this. On the one hand there is an obvious need to find two
actors with sufficient experience to master the complexities of
difficult roles while of course convincingly playing teenagers;
the Nurse is quite explicit about Juliet's youth and Romeo
must be little older. Actors rarely come to the parts much
younger than 25 and have often been as old as 35. Yet this is
often a technicality; what matters most is that Romeo and
Juliet must complement one another. In 1961 Dorothy Tutin
created a Juliet of great emotional intensity and romantic
appeal but there was never any sense of an instant deep
passion between her and her Romeo, played by Brian Murray. Niamh Cusack, who played Juliet in Michael Bogdanov's
1986 production, has spoken of the need to audition the two
main characters as a pair, to test the balance of their
relationship:

We meet only five times in the play and if the audience doesn't believe utterly in our love then the whole thing is a waste of time.   (*Players of Shakespeare 2*, 1988, p. 123)

In order to explore the issues outlined above, the following discussion focuses specifically upon five modern productions: 1961 at the Old Vic Theatre, directed by Franco Zeffirelli, with John Stride and Judi Dench as Romeo and Juliet and four productions by the Royal Shakespeare Company, in 1973, directed by Terry Hands, with Timothy Dalton and Estelle Kohler; 1976, directed by Trevor Nunn and Barry Kyle, with Ian McKellen and Francesca Annis; 1986, directed by Michael Bogdanov, with Sean Bean and Niamh Cusack and 1989, directed by Terry Hands, with Mark Rylance and Georgia Slowe. Reference is also made to a number of other productions: 1961, directed by Peter Hall, with Dorothy Tutin and Brian Murray; 1967, directed by Karolos Koun, with Estelle Kohler and Ian Holm; 1980, directed by Ron Daniels, with Anton Lesser and Judy Buxton and 1984 (after a 1983 tour), directed by John Caird, with Simon Templeman and Amanda Root.

7   FRANCO ZEFFIRELLI, OLD VIC THEATRE, 1961

Zeffirelli was asked to direct *Romeo and Juliet* largely as a result of his recent work at Covent Garden. The management of the Old Vic was attracted as much by his talents as a designer of atmospheric Italian settings for *Cavalleria Rusticana* as by his skills as a director. Zeffirelli set about stripping away the accretions of outdated romantic conventions of acting and staging in an attempt to bring the play to life for a modern, primarily young, audience. His aim was to achieve a feeling of naturalism, essentially by providing appropriate visual expression to Shakespeare's text.

In some respects Zeffirelli returned to the elaborate scenery of the nineteenth century in order to achieve the vitality for which the production became famous. At times the scenery represented specific locations in details that superficially remind one of the efforts of Henry Irving. However, Zeffirelli and the designer, Peter Hall, created scenery that was both beautiful (based on Veronese frescoes) and believable, blending muted earth colours with subtle lighting effects. More important, Zeffirelli avoided the lengthy delays that are associated with elaborate scenery by using only three basic sets: one that displayed ochre-coloured walls that could be transformed easily into interior scenes, one for the balcony and one for the final tomb scene. The opening scene, bathed in the stark, harsh white light of noon-day Italy and the balcony scene, lit with muted shadows, were notably successful. Juliet's bedchamber scene, as she prepares to take the Friar's sleeping potion, was less successful simply because, by using a single lurid red spotlight focused on the bed, the director limited both Juliet's movement and the range of emotion she was able to express. In addition to scenic design, Zeffirelli lavished astonishing care in meticulously working out actions that gave precise expression to many of the lines of the text. As John Russell Brown has observed of the production:

> The greatest innovation of his production lay in unifying words and stage-business, in making the actors' speech as lively and fluent as their physical action. The result was that dialogue did not appear the effect of study and care, but the natural idiom of the characters in the particular situations.
>
> ('S. Franco Zeffirelli's *Romeo and Juliet*', p. 149)

Zeffirelli was perhaps equally innovative in his decisions regarding the appearance and costume of the characters. Gone was the tradition of moody romantic beauty for the central characters. In its place the characters were dressed in muted colours that genuinely gave the impression that they were to be worn everyday. Even more importantly, gone also was every trace of actors striking attitudes. The balcony scene provides a striking illustration. Zeffirelli set the balcony unusually high, perhaps five metres above the stage, so that Romeo's attempts to reach Juliet were genuinely thwarted by the distance that separated the two lovers. Romeo clambered up a tree that flanked one side of the balcony and reached in vain to touch Juliet's outstretched fingertips. The sense of tension and straining to overcome physical limitations may seem an obvious directorial touch, but it proved electrifying. Zeffirelli departed from a tradition that can be seen in engravings of productions such as that at Covent Garden in the middle of the eighteenth-century in which Spranger Barry, who played Romeo, can be seen striking an elegant pose beneath the balcony, appropriately commended by a contemporary for its tenderness and eloquence (the picture is reproduced in Evans's New Cambridge edition, p. 38). Indeed, many modern directors have struggled to define precisely the correct distance between the two lovers in this scene and failure to gauge correctly has resulted in comedy or loss of emotional intensity. Zeffirelli's efforts were always intended to increase the impression of spontaneity; not surprisingly the production was most notably successful in the first half of the play and especially in a series of key moments of heightened emotional intensity. These included the street fights and, of course, the balcony scene. The fight between Mercutio and Tybalt was cleared of the formality of a duel and instead the action followed the rapid exaggerated taunts of the text.

One consequence of Zeffirelli's approach was that poetry often seemed to be subordinate to action. Although the production was startling in this respect, there was important precedent, particularly in a highly influential Old Vic production which played at the New Theatre in 1935. Then Laurence Olivier and John Gielgud had alternated the roles of Mercutio and Romeo; but it was Olivier's performance that first freed the role of Romeo from its artificiality. Olivier strove for realism by being deliberately unpoetical, finding poetry in action rather than verse. He described his approach as one of 'carrying a torch ... trying to sell realism in Shakespeare', contrasting his efforts in the role to Gielgud's music and lyricism (quoted in Richard David, *Shakespeare in the Theatre*, 1978, p. 232). However, if anything Zeffirelli went much further than this, and as Judi Dench, who played Juliet was later to recall, often the director simply 'forgot the poetry'. Zeffirelli himself was even more forthright at the time; 'verse speakers will be prosecuted' was his command during rehearsals (quoted in an interview with Gareth Lloyd Evans in

Shakespeare Survey 27, 1974, p. 138). As a result the production achieved astonishing vitality and immediacy but often at a significant cost, particularly in the second half of the play.

Zeffirelli demanded an extraordinary degree of both physical and emotional energy from the two central characters. Both Stride and Dench were young and utterly convincing as teenagers. Dench, tiny in stature and with a round-faced, wide-eyed beauty and Stride, with his tousled brown hair and dressed in what seemed to be a tweed material, were more English than Italian lovers, but the energy and physical awkwardness of youthful love were certainly present in their performances.

Zeffirelli's treatment of the verse meant that both characters delivered their speeches with no trace of affectation. However, at times this was achieved at what many viewers considered a high price, with some lines garbled or inaudible. There were intelligent liberties taken with key scenes: Romeo's departure into exile (III v) was staged on a large four-poster bed, in which the two lovers lay in apparent exhaustion after their wedding night. At times in rehearsals the two central actors fought to retain the rhythmic, more formal delivery that their English training had instilled and the struggle took its toll both on the actors (Dench was so exhausted by her efforts in the production that she left the production when it went on a worldwide tour, to be replaced by Joanna Dunham) and on the audience. Juliet's soliloquy before taking the potion was broken up into fragments in order to emphasize a series of discrete emotions, an effect heightened by physical actions as Dench writhed in emotional anguish on the bed; as a result the speech lost coherence and left the audience more confused than moved by what they witnessed. At times naturalism seemed self-defeating, as in moments of extreme grief, when the lovers were required to accompany their actions with the physical contortions of children. Dench was later to recall how much the experience had taught her about 'non-classical passion, about real hot-blooded passion' but the fact was that at times such contortions conflicted with the verse. For instance, in III iii, Romeo's passionate outburst on hearing of his banishment depends for its effect upon relatively complex rhetorical links, developing images of corruption and purity and returning to the key word 'banish'. By striving for a sense of the purely spontaneous in such a speech, Stride conveyed only a generalized sense of incoherent grief. Nowhere was this danger more evident than in the final act, discussed below.

McCowen played the part of Mercutio with the same high-spirits exhibited by the two central characters. His behaviour was that of a clown, an irrepressible joker whose jesting and buffoonery were the natural adjuncts to a young man determined to hold centre-stage at every moment. The Queen Mab speech was given much the same treatment as has been described for Juliet's soliloquy before taking the potion. The lines were broken into a series of images, delivered with utter spontaneity. Zeffirelli explained in an interview for *Stage and Television Today* (13 October 1960) that he did not feel that there was anything 'notable in a poetic sense' in the speech. Once again the result was exciting but struck some viewers as incoherent. Perhaps most significantly, under Zeffirelli's direction McCowen created a Mercutio who did not compete with Romeo as the romantic hero. Instead he combined wit and intellect and, above all, energy.

McCowen's behaviour in Mercutio's fatal duel with Tybalt most clearly demonstrates his innovative approach to the part. Exhibiting no skill as a duelist, he instead chose to respond to Tybalt's threats as though they were a joke, simply one more opportunity to delight his audience of youthful Mantuans. Rather than an exhibition of skilful Elizabethan swordplay between two angry and aristocratic men, the scene was played as grotesque comedy, turning bitter purely by chance. More than anything else, the fight was entirely lacking in chivalry; it was wild, undisciplined, entirely indecorous.

Perhaps the greatest benefit of this approach to the role was that Mercutio's death did not dangerously unbalance the play in the way that can often be the case. His death indeed marks a turning point in the play but it must primarily be one of lost exhuberance, rather than a loss of romantic interest to rival Romeo. When Olivier had played the role to John Gielgud's Romeo in 1935 he had often seemed to rival him as a swaggering hero and so his death marked all too clearly the loss of one of the twin centres of the play. Such a performance

can make the gap from first half joy to last-act doom too great
to traverse.

The final scene exposed the weakness of Zeffirelli's
approach most glaringly, or at least demonstrated the extent
to which the director was willing to distort the text in order to
press the play in certain specific directions. He made the
development in Romeo's character almost impossible for
Stride to convey, by concentrating upon a distracted anger in
the exchange with the Apothecary, excluding any opportunity
for the actor to suggest the extent to which Romeo has a
new-found resolution in his grief. In the last scene Zeffirelli
followed in a long line of directors, reaching back to the
adaptations of the late seventeenth century, who have refused,
or been unable, to accommodate the formality of the last
hundred or so lines, from Juliet's death to the end of the play.
Zeffirelli simply cut almost everything after Juliet's death,
retaining only the last fifteen lines, from the Prince's 'Where
be these enemies?' In place of the missing lines Zeffirelli
substituted a series of elaborate silent gestures, grouping
characters in poses of reconciliation and grief. In so doing the
production eliminated Shakespeare's final emphasis upon the
rituals of public grief in which, as John Russell Brown has
said, 'responsibility is learnt in adversity'. John Stride's
assessment of both his own and the director's attitude to the
last scenes is particularly telling. Recalling a series of debates
over cuts made by Zeffirelli to the beginning of Act v, Stride
described the director's attitude as 'merciless . . . because he
was trying to do a cinematic cut, and as the play got towards
the end, he tried to do more and more of these, since he didn't
understand — and indeed, neither did I'. One of Zeffirelli's
additions to the series of actions that ended the play indicates
most clearly the extent to which he had failed to understand
something central to the play. With the bodies occupying
centre stage the survivors began silently to take their exits.
The two families gathered at opposite sides of the tomb and
left from separate exits without giving even a glance across at
their former enemies, let alone any signs of reconciliation.
Zeffirelli thereby kept the death of the two lovers rigidly at the
centre of attention and allowed no real scope for any channel-
ling of the grief into public gestures. As a result, Zeffirelli

forced the audience to settle for sentimentality rather than
Shakespeare's far more complicated mixture of emotions.

8   TERRY HANDS, RSC, 1973

'These violent delights have violent ends' was printed in bold
type across the centre page of the programme and seemed to
have been Terry Hands' central text in planning this production. Almost every detail contributed to its robust energy,
from the opening street scene, with a naked flame burning
high on an upstage wall creating a sense of foreboding before
an opening explosion of exhilarating violence, to the enthu-
siasm with which Juliet passed the time while waiting for the
Nurse's return with a message from Romeo by beating the
carpets hung from clotheslines cluttering the stage. This was a
production in which it was abundantly clear that the director
intended to dispel any illusions of joyful romance. Several key
directorial and design decisions dominated the production
and clearly influenced the actors.

   The set, designed by Farrah, was forbiddingly brutal, with
huge sliding steel towers, one on each side of stage. These
towers each supported an open stairway, leading up to a metal
bridge that spanned the stage and served as the balcony. The
set dwarfed the characters and allowed little opportunity for
the expression of tenderness, particularly in interior scenes.
There could be little doubt that the two lovers were doomed
from the start, and that the source of the tragedy lay outside
their character. Fair Verona was transformed into a maze of
scaffolding, setting the tone for a production that aimed from
the outset to be extrovert, emphasizing speed and violence
rather than romance. Unfortunately the set seemed to influence the acoustics so that, in the balcony scenes in particular, Juliet was almost inaudible as well as being visibly
trapped by the gangway on which she stood. The costumes
were vaguely Jacobean but with a strong emphasis upon a
rather clumsy bulkiness which also contributed to an overall

sense of brutality as well as occasionally making the actors' movements seem rather clumsy.

The other significant features were similarly unsubtle, although less overwhelming than the set. At every appearance Mercutio carried a life-sized female doll, which he used to exaggerated effect to illustrate his sexual innuendo. During the 'invocation' scene (II i) he publicly dismembered the doll, lending a grotesque and disturbing violence to his feverish joking at Rosaline's expense. Hands also chose to stage key scenes beneath the brooding presence of an anonymous hooded and bearded figure on the balcony, who was present throughout much of the second half of the play. The figure, who appeared whenever the action emphasized the lover's impending doom, eventually entered the action as the Apothecary. Intended as a reminder of inexorable fate, in fact the figure seemed to act as a distraction and made a nonsense of Shakespeare's careful indication that the Apothecary is also an innocent victim. Curiously, in a production that tended to suggest that fate was a product of environment rather than character, the Apothecary, victim of neglect and poverty, seemed a lost opportunity by being presented exclusively as the brooding personification of fate. His appearance at the very beginning of the play, standing aloof at the very highest point above the stage, was a particularly heavy-handed directorial touch which was out of keeping with the otherwise effective staging in which the cast moved onto the stage in dumb show while the Prince presented the opening chorus-sonnet.

Given a setting of such aggressive ugliness, dressed in drab homespun costumes and surrounded by a supporting cast who seemed determined to develop every opportunity for violence, energy and bawdry, it was clear that the central characters would be required to play against the text's lyricism. In the event Estelle Kohler's Juliet proved much more successful than Timothy Dalton as Romeo.

Kohler had already played Juliet for the RSC in a 1967 production with the Greek director Karolos Koun. In the earlier production Koun had deliberately emphasized the tragedy of fate and Kohler had been a notable success. In 1967 she conveyed Juliet's youthful impetuous energy and innocence in a performance that elicited powerful audience sympathy.

Although the 1973 production was similarly doom-laden, Kohler made no attempt to play Juliet as a passive teenager, nor to prettify the role. This resulted in some confusion, particularly in her opening scene, I iii. As the Nurse launched into her lengthy reminiscence of Juliet's infancy, mother and daughter sat side by side, stifling laughter which burst forth at the Nurse's bawdy joke:

> 'Yea', quoth he, 'dost thou fall upon thy face?
> Thou wit fall backward when thou hast more wit,
> Wilt thou not, Jule?'   (I iii 42–4)

The laughter suggested the shared awareness of two adult women, unembarrassed by their sexuality and amused by the servant who was playing to her audience. Such an exchange made the sudden shift to passivity more than a little confusing. Juliet's 'I'll look to like, if looking liking move' (I iii 98–100) seemed more like a cautious equivocation than the conventional response of a dutiful Elizabethan daughter.

However, Kohler was much more effective in those scenes that allowed full reign to passionate emotions, and was notably successful in the second half of the play. She dominated the balcony scene and seemed in clear control in arranging the marriage. Kohler is an actress with a powerful voice, open expressive face and evident physical strength. This was demonstrated with tremendous vitality in the already-mentioned scene in which she anticipated the return of her nurse with a message from Romeo. In staging this scene Hands used a telling domestic detail. Large carpets were hung on clotheslines that were strung across the width of the stage. In her impatience Juliet passed the time by beating the carpets with characteristic energy. This Juliet was certainly not a passive victim of fate. With her long, unkempt hair streaming round her face she was equally memorable in her later exchange, in IV i, with Friar Laurence. At first she was barely able to disguise her contempt for Paris, then after his departure she unleashed a tirade of passionate defiance against her fate:

> I long to die
> If what thou speak'st speak not of remedy.
>   (IV i 66–7)

Despite her obvious energy, Kohler's performance was not
exclusively extroverted. Having demonstrated the strength
and maturity of her passionate nature, her reaction to the
Nurse's advice that she forget Romeo and marry Paris was
memorable for its silent self-absorption. Kohler held a long
pause as she registered the Nurse's betrayal and began to
measure the extent of her utter isolation. Her next line was
less a response than an interior monologue, uttered in an
almost inaudible monotone:

> *Juliet:* Speakest thou from thy heart?
> *Nurse:* And from my soul too, else beshrew them both.
> *Juliet:* Amen.

(III v 227–9)

It was a moment of utter devastation, marking a convincing
turning point as Juliet then embarked upon a series of
desperate actions.

The strength of Kohler's performance rather unbalanced
the relationship with Timothy Dalton as Romeo. Dalton
certainly looked the part of a romantic youth, and played the
role with athletic grace. However, in scenes that provided no
opportunity for activity he seemed lost and his rather light
tenor voice was ill-suited to either lyricism or depths of
emotion. Curiously, where Kohler developed Juliet's emotional depths in the last half of the play, Dalton was most
convincing in the first half. As an adolescent, experimenting
with his own emotions for Rosaline in the bookish clichés of
Petrarch, and as the enraged killer of Tybalt he was entirely
convincing but during the latter half of the play he often
seemed merely to rant and rage. The final cry of anguish over
Juliet's dead body was particularly disappointing, almost
thrown away by Dalton's inability to convey the depths of a
lover's emotions. His difficulties in the role were exacerbated
by the curious relationship between Romeo and Mercutio.
Although Bernard Lloyd's performance as Mercutio was striking and one of the most memorable features of the production,
its very strength tended to disturb the play's balance. Romeo's
early infatuation with Rosaline seemed impossibly naive by
contrast to his friend's extravagant worldliness, and rather

than gentle mockery the overall impression was that his rather artificial language was being savagely pilloried.

As with much else in this production, Lloyd played Mercutio with savage energy and little subtlety. The performance was dominated by the fact that he constantly carried a grotesque, coarse-featured, life-size female doll, upon which he vented a clearly sado-masochistic sexual loathing. 'Here are the beetle brows shall blush for me' (I iv 32) was turned into a reference to the doll and constituted a scornful rejection of feminine tenderness leading up to a graphic, deeply-disturbed and equally disturbing, dismemberment of the doll. His violence was barely contained from the start, so that his initial exchanges with Romeo seemed less a matter of the lively banter of youthful equals than the baiting of an increasingly isolated sociopath. Every opportunity for sexual innuendo was followed by an obscene gesture, setting the tone for much of the early all-male exchanges. The long Queen Mab speech was accompanied by similarly explicit gestures and with an extraordinary sense of pacing. The climax was frenzied and quite terrifying:

> This is the hag, when maids lie on their backs,
> That presses them and learns them first to bear,
> Making them women of good carriage.
> This is she –
> Romeo: Peace, peace, Mercutio, peace.
> Thou talkest of nothing.

(I iv 92–6)

At this point Mercutio sat almost apoplectic on the ground, quite oblivious of his embarrassed friends. Romeo's lines thus became the soothing intervention of an old friend to one who is deeply disturbed. The focus shifted completely on to sexual loathing, quite eclipsing the more subtle possibilities inherent in the speech. Although the scene was electrifying, it certainly narrowed the dimensions of Mercutio's fear of the imagination. There was no attempt to suggest what lay behind the character's aberrant psychology, aside perhaps from some quite unspecified and unexplained misogyny. However, the performance was certainly consistent with the emphasis upon violence, the austere set and the doom-laden atmosphere of the rest of the production. Of more fundamental importance to the play, Lloyd's performance changed the significance of Romeo's affection and seemed to restrict his opportunities to indicate the character's emotional development.

Perhaps the most affecting moment in the production came in the scene of lament by Capulet and his household over the apparently dead body of Juliet. It is a moment in which the text demands a degree of ritual formality in order to control an exchange that runs perilously close to parody, as a segment of the Nurse's contribution suggests:

> O woe! O woeful, woeful, woeful day!
> Most lamentable day, most woeful day
> That ever, ever did yet behold!
> O day, O day, O day! O hateful day!
> Never was seen so black a day as this.
>   (IV v 49–53)

The lines are remarkably close to the Pyramus and Thisbe death scenes in *A Midsummer Night's Dream* and were given an almost operatic treatment by Hands. Successive speakers picked up the tone of lament from their predecessor, overlapping with some of the final phrases and then developing the cry with appropriate personal embellishments. The emotion of the lament was sincere but kept at a certain distance, while allowing the audience simultaneously to enjoy the fact that of course Juliet was still alive. The play's comic potential cleverly resurfaced for a final brief moment, to be lost in the succeeding rush of events.

The final scene was played with the same blunt energy that had characterized the rest of the production. Played in near darkness, the scene was perhaps the one most suited to the grim set and the overwhelming atmosphere of doom. To a great extent, therefore, the scene succeeded simply because Hands was at last able to take full advantage of the charnel house mood that had been dominant throughout. However, the absence of any variation of tone inevitably restricted the impact of the final lines of the play, once the two lovers were dead. Indeed, Dalton's tendency to play every opportunity for emotion at full scream diminished Romeo's great death scene, simply because it precluded any attempt to explore the scene's undertones of romance and eroticism. Weeping over the prostrate body of Juliet, he turned his final speech into a near-falsetto shriek of anguish, which clashed oddly with the repeated references to exhaustion and world-weariness that precede the suicide.

The production had concentrated almost exclusively upon animation and energetic pacing, and in the last lines, following Juliet's death, the cast seemed somewhat at a loss. Almost 60 lines were cut, with deletions focusing upon the entry of the watchman and the bustle of activity that precedes and accompanies the entries of the Prince and the lovers' parents. As a result there was no transition period from the deaths to the ritualistic formality of the final hundred lines. Instead, the families gathered round the bodies, to await a reconciliation that seemed curiously inappropriate. Somehow, amid the frenetic energy, the crude bawdry, the presiding spectral figure of the Apothecary and the overwhelming harshness of the set, there seemed in the end to be no room for even the Prince's 'glooming peace'. Juliet's body was steeped in a quite extravagant quantity of blood, and it was this, rather than the possibility of golden statues, that seemed the more fitting memorial to the preceding events.

9   TREVOR NUNN AND BARRY KYLE, RSC, 1976

In 1976 the management of the Royal Shakespeare Company took a deliberate artistic decision to use a single fixed set, designed by John Napier and Chris Dyer, that did as much as possible to transform Stratford's large, essentially proscenium-arch auditorium into something approximating to an Elizabethan stage. In fact the management denied that they had any thoughts of the seventeenth-century stage in mind, claiming instead that they had simply sought to create a simple, fluid acting space. In the end this amounted to much the same thing, as most audiences were aware. The front of the stage was built out into the auditorium to give something of the

effect of a thrust stage and two wooden-framed tiers, contain-
ing bench seats for spectators, were constructed to encircle the
back of the stage. The result was a nearly circular acting area,
with the audience virtually all round the stage. The balcony
for *Romeo and Juliet* was simply an extension that blended into
the centre of the tiers. Nothing cluttered the bare stage aside
from a few movable props such as beds and stools. Costumes
were loosely Jacobean, with the exception of the Chorus, who
was dressed incongruously in modern casual attire. Few
lighting effects were attempted. Instead a range of spotlights,
which filled the area over the stage, was as a rule simply used
to flood the stage with light: the interior equivalent of after-
noon sun.

Although the stage was therefore close in appearance to
what is known of Shakespeare's contemporary theatres, there
were a number of technical difficulties. There were only seats
for approximately 70 people at the back of the acting area,
and, presumably unlike the approach taken in Shakespeare's
theatre, little of the action was directed towards them. More
significantly, the stage design could not overcome the fact that
in the large, rectangular, Stratford auditorium some of the
audience is seated at a much greater distance than would ever
have been the case in Shakespeare's theatre. In fact, the
additional upstage tiers distorted the acoustics of the auditorium and seem to have made hearing even more difficult for
some in the audience. The end result was a superficial
authenticity that initially masked and then ultimately aggra-
vated the accustomed lack of intimacy in a large, essentially
nineteenth-century auditorium. The directors, Trevor Nunn
and Barry Kyle, struggled to overcome these difficulties in a
production that concentrated upon the youthful sincerity and
passion of the central characters.

The perennial difficulties in casting a mature actor to play a
teenager weighed heavily upon Ian McKellen in his performance as Romeo. McKellen overcompensated for the fact that
he was in his mid-thirties, resorting to every possible manner-
ism and affectation in order to suggest a youthful Romeo.
Although McKellen already had a youthful face, he added a
boyishly curled hair style, which was ludicrously emphasized
in the early scenes by the fact that he bound a kerchief round

his head. For the first half of the play Romeo was always fluttering about the stage, with what was intended to be a youthful grin on his face, a grimace which more often seemed a grotesque parody of youth. In the balcony scene he sighed and flapped his arms in what was meant to be youthful abandon. Romeo's sentimental ecstasy depends absolutely upon the audience being convinced of its sincerity, otherwise the perfervid poetry degenerates into mere comedy. Unfortunately, McKellen sighed, grimaced and, when he explained that he had entered the garden with 'love's light wings', he flapped his long arms as though ready to fly. By drawing excessive attention to the bookish artifice of the verse, McKellen destroyed the delicate balance of the scene. His affectations were less evident later in the play but could resurface at odd moments. Richard David, in *Shakespeare in the Theatre* (1978), transcribed McKellen's cry of defiance after hearing news of Juliet's death from Balthasar as 'Then I defy – YOOHOO STARS!' (p. 117) which is a fair indication of the extent of the actor's excesses.

Francesca Annis was altogether more convincing as a shy teenager. Annis is a delicate, almost frail actress, with a fine-featured face, pale skin and light voice. When she giggled and gambolled about the stage in her early scenes, or when she reached timidly to touch Romeo's hand, 'palm to palm' for the first time, her childish self-absorption was entirely credible. As John Barber observed when describing the production in the *Daily Telegraph*, McKellen 'imitated the mannerisms of youth' while Annis 'came much closer to its ardent spirit'. However, there were compensations to McKellen's approach. The shift from youthful infatuation with Rosaline to love for Juliet was marked by a gradual dropping of affected expression and exaggerated movement as Juliet exerted a quiet influence.

Mary Keane played the Nurse as an intelligent confidante with a fine Irish-accented earthiness. The performance was carefully controlled and disappointed some, who missed the bravura acting of earlier representations of the part, but it provided a credible domestic context for Juliet's early skittishness. Curiously, perhaps the greatest indication of the success with which Keane played a supporting role is the fact that she made so little impact on audience and critics alike. The scene in which Juliet finally shuts her out was muted, perhaps lacking in pathos, but in this production there was no risk that the Nurse would steal a scene.

The sense of overwhelming loss at the end of the play was particularly strong in this production, beginning with Capulet's frenzied incomprehension on finding his daughter dead on her marriage day. Finding his daughter still in bed he erupted in rage, shaking and flinging her frail body to the floor, before collapsing in mute agony at her side. Perhaps of most importance, the elegaic mood of the long final scene was almost completely successful, as will be seen in the discussion below.

Michael Pennington was an extravagantly humorous Mercutio whose behaviour seemed dominated by an inability to avoid playing to the crowd of youthful spectators who seemed to hang on his every move. He skipped, winked, hopped and fluttered with a knowing leer that made Romeo's behaviour seem all the more naive; at one point he capped a jest by thrusting out his bottom toward Romeo in a gesture that was as much a schoolboyish flouting of propriety as it was a sign of repressed homosexual attraction. The frenetic energy of the production's early scenes and his own constant exhausting comic routines precluded the development of any deeper relationship between Mercutio and Romeo; instead Mercutio in particular seemed in constant competition to outshine his friend. His hatred for Tybalt's affectations was apparently born out of rivalry, as he was easily more fantastic than the 'antic lisping affecting phantasime' he claimed to despise. Similarly, the Queen Mab speech was played as a comic tour-de-force but one which was delivered with an almost lackadaisical sense of pacing, almost entirely lacking any sense that the character was becoming progressively more enmeshed in his own fantasies. For all his humorous insistence that 'love' should always be conceived in purely physical terms, this Mercutio was almost entirely lacking in any sense of the mystery of an unacknowledged and fertile imagination.

Mercutio's death was perhaps the most poignant moment in the play, a tragedy in which Mercutio simply miscalculated the mood of his opponent. The duel was incredibly fast, an exhilarating competition in which Mercutio managed repeatedly to deflect danger with a joke. His death came as he leapt into Tybalt's arms to plant a mocking kiss, and his final lines, far from a cry of rage, seemed more the anger of a clown whose best joke has been spoilt by the bad timing of his straight man. He was dragged from the stage, fixing Romeo with a ghastly smile.

Pennington's performance perfectly illustrated the character's inconsistencies. His humour was not simply a curious distraction from the central event; it was instead seen to be an integral feature. One of the great successes of this production, achieved to a great extent thanks to Pennington's Mercutio, was that it consistently managed to convince the audience that laughter and sorrow, life and death were always in close company.

Having taken the decision to use a fixed set without any added scenery, the directors had to face the problem of staging the final scene without an enclosure for the tomb. The solution was simple, and largely effective, demonstrating that the modern audience is quite capable of full imaginative engagement with the text. The final scene was heavily, but selectively cut, with elisions apparently primarily focused to achieve several specific goals. Given the absence of a tomb, the directors decided to remove certain fairly obvious opportunities for confusion, such as Romeo's reference to Tybalt lying in his bloody sheet. Indeed, the body was never seen. Instead, Romeo and Paris both simply appeared, equipped with crowbars, on the balcony above the stage beneath which Juliet lay. Approach to the tomb was achieved by climbing down and then proceeding to prise open the trap door, located downstage. Once he had killed Paris, Romeo simply dragged the body near to the trap before opening it and lifting Juliet's limp body out from beneath. Aside from this staging difficulty other cuts reduced the audience's engagement with Paris as a sympathetic figure by significantly reducing his opening elegy.

Romeo's death (v iii 85–120) was accompanied by a small piece of directorial genius, an interpolated action that served to heighten the audience's awareness of how close the tragedy is at this point to happiness. McKellen dropped all traces of his earlier affectations, delivering 'Shall I believe/That unsubstantial Death is amorous' with quiet restraint. The last few lines, from 'seal with a righteous kiss' to his death, were delivered almost joyously, more epithalamium than elegy. McKellen lifted Annis's tiny figure in his arms, wrapping her limp arms round his neck, and stood her upright while still supporting her. The upright position heightened the irony by reminding the audience that the apparent mockery of life was in fact within moments of the truth. McKellen then sat down with his feet in the open hole of the tomb, still cradling Juliet's body in his arms. Romeo's final kiss was passionate, even erotic; as he kissed Juliet, her hand fluttered with the first signs of returning life, unseen by Romeo but in full view of the audience. At Romeo's death the promptbook specifies a touch that captured both the tenderness and the horror of the scene: 'Juliet falls on top of him, hand falls touching his face'.

The last 100 lines of the play succeeded primarily as a result of the fact that John Woodvine had earlier played Capulet with the restrained violence of an old bully used to having his own way in his own household. This was most notable in the opening scene, in which he was seen to be perfectly capable of wielding a sword and, in Act IV, in his violent rage when Juliet had refused to marry Paris. Having earlier demonstrated the extent to which he was a character dominated by instant emotions, it was consistent that in the final scene he should initially try to vent his anger by kicking Romeo's limp corpse and by attempting to turn Juliet's dagger on the bumbling friar. However, it was his quiet collapse at the end of the play that gave full weight to the final lines:

> O brother Montague, give me thy hand.
> This is my daughter's jointure, for no more
> Can I demand.   (v iii 296–8)

These lines were delivered in a hollow monotone, which brought to life the full impact of his daughter's death upon a proud and energetic man. In Capulet's voice and face could be sensed a desolation that no public reconciliation or golden monuments could possibly compensate. The Chorus, rather than Prince Escalus, then spoke the final four lines of the play, a change that was largely gratuitous, although it added a nice symmetry to the play, ending as it had begun, with an anonymous spokesman. The sombre ending was in stark contrast to the lightheartedness of much of the earlier portions of the play. Indeed the wholehearted acceptance of this contrast, and the refusal to deny the joy and frivolity of much that occurs in the first half, constituted the production's greatest strength.

10   MICHAEL BOGDANOV, RSC, 1986/7

The design by Chris Dyer for Michael Bogdanov's production signalled one of the most striking and challenging attempts to lend the play an overt modernity. Apparently constructed of white marble and chrome, the set was all harsh angles and sharp edges, with a central area of open staircases and landings. This revolving centre piece was backed by constantly changing photographic blow-ups of modern society figures and fragments of modern architecture. The set even incorporated a swimming pool. Every detail was aggressively modern, from policemen on motorcycles wearing sunglasses, to a buzzing intercom for Capulet's marble desk and to the fashionable Italian-design modern clothing worn by the cast. The fight scene between Mercutio and Tybalt contained the most striking example of the often flippant nature of this drive to establish the play's modernity. This duel began as a display of machismo and bluff and was only precipitated into genuine anger once Mercutio scratched Tybalt's sports car – inevitably, a gleaming Alfa Romeo.

Against this modern backdrop the characters were played as recognizable modern types: teenage gang members, Italian business tycoons, a nurse with social aspirations. As a result the production had immense vitality, coupled with a great deal of uncertainty at its heart, forcing Shakespeare's complex roles toward stereotypes. At times the effort to find modern counterparts for Elizabethan characters and actions was excessively literal-minded and resulted in clumsy gimmickry. The fights took place with chains and flick knives rather than rapiers; Capulet's ball took the form of a swinging sixties party complete with rock music and, inevitably, a much applauded fall into the swimming pool. Romeo killed himself with an injection from a hypodermic syringe. The original intention, according to Niamh Cusack, who played Juliet, was that she should commit suicide by shooting herself, although this idea was scrapped in rehearsal. Amid this clutter of superficial modernity, the two lovers often had to struggle to avoid appearing like characters from *West Side Story*.

Describing her performance as Juliet in this production in *Players of Shakespeare 2* (1988), Niamh Cusack demonstrates a fine sensitivity to the demands of the role by insisting upon the fact that the two central characters must complement one another perfectly. In approaching the part, she says, she realized that:

> My Juliet could not exist as it is without Sean Bean's Romeo; I see our relationship, above all in the balcony scene, through him.
> ... I feel that the Romeo I play against serves my Juliet one hundred per cent in the vulnerability and total commitment of his playing of a young boy in love.
>
> (pp. 122–23)

Setting the play in such a modern context caused Cusack certain difficulties in finding credible motivation for some of her early actions, as did the shift in tone from first half joy to later tragedy:

> One aspect, for example, that emerged only later is the joyous side of her personality at the beginning. I was rather afraid of that at first, in case it should diminish the tragic ending, but of course the more you go for the early joy, the more powerful is the contrasting impact of the final tragedy.
>
> (p. 123)

In order to make sense of the early scenes in a modern setting it was necessary to heighten the distance between Juliet and her mother. In fact there was no sense of a relationship between the two at all. Juliet's joyous character emerged despite the coldness of a socialite mother and the attentions of a sycophantic nurse. Dilys Laye played the Nurse as a brandy swilling opportunist, a smartly dressed, middle-aged woman,

hoping to ride the coat tails of her rather crass parvenu
employer, Lady Capulet. When, in III v, she suddenly turns
into an advocate for a marriage with Paris, her behaviour was
not particularly dictated by the pressure of circumstances or a
desperate desire to see her beloved Juliet happy. It was the
natural expression of a woman used to seizing opportunities
when they came. The key note was less that Juliet might be
'happy in this second match' but that 'it excels the first'. The
production skewed Shakespeare's carefully constructed social
context and almost totally removed the Nurse's vital function
as confidante, but it did manage to suggest a believable reason
for Juliet's early loneliness and later self-reliance.

Both of the central characters were played by young and
relatively inexperienced actors and, as Romeo, Sean Bean
looked a perfect match to Juliet. The pair shared an open-eyed
innocence and the production managed to convey a powerful
sense of sexual attraction. However, Bean lacked the vocal
range to cope with the role. The early Petrarchan oxymora
were garbled and heavily delivered, completely lacking the
schoolboy delight in verbal dexterity that is so evident in the
early exchanges with Mercutio. Indeed, there was little sense
throughout of either Romeo's hyperbolic imagination or lyricism. Here was a bluff Romeo of little subtlety, best in
moments of blunt honest emotion.

As with everything else about the production, the characters fared best when releasing the play's latent comedy. This
meant that the first half had a good deal of robust energy but,
as will be seen in the following discussion of the final scene,
the tragedy of the second half was lost beneath an oppressive
weight of gimmickry and subsumed within a director's desire
to exploit Shakespeare in order to make rather superficial
topical points.

Mercutio's death scene in 1986 resembled the approach
taken in 1976 by playing the duel largely as a joke. Michael
Kitchen teased Hugh Quarshie, who played Tybalt, by
prancing up and down the stairs that occupied centre-stage,
taunting and staying just out of reach. At one point there was
a pause as Kitchen mimed a practice golf swing with his
walking stick and the entire action froze as Mercutio appeared
to damage Tybalt's precious car. The scene was often hilari-

ous, especially when Quarshie looked with incoherent rage for the scratch on the car.

However, where Michael Pennington had played Mercutio as a mercurial fantastic, Kitchen rooted his characterization in the boorish verbosity of a streetwise drunken lout. His drunkenness removed the character's intelligence and wit, suggesting that the constant banter was little more than slurred alcoholic ramblings. At his death Mercutio pretended to run out of breath and, from 'villain, go fetch a surgeon' on, he delivered his last words in a quickly mumbled gabble, the irascible drunk robbed of his life and unable to sober up enough to confront his fate.

It was a fundamentally misconceived approach, dictated by the production's relentless drive to find modern counterparts for Elizabethan characters. Although the approach lent some straightforward credibility to his erratic behaviour and verbosity, it made it extremely difficult for any audience to believe that he and Romeo were anything more than drinking companions, or to comprehend Romeo's extraordinary anger at his death. Similarly, the Queen Mab speech was delivered with a camp clumsiness, with Mercutio taking Romeo on his lap to deliver a lengthy homily, and thereby shutting off any opportunity of exploring beneath the surface of the speech.

Bogdanov's direction of the final scene was consistent with his emphasis throughout the play upon modernity and upon the intolerable pressures that can still affect youthful love. As such, the final scene illustrates perfectly both the compensations and the limitations of a production in which everything is pressed into the service of a single central idea.

The scene was heavily cut. In the 200 lines up until the death of Juliet the cuts were relatively unobtrusive, primarily intended to remove opportunities for confusion, such as Paris's reference (lines 30–2) to a ring that he has come to retrieve from Juliet's body. The cuts also tended to reduce audience interest, and sympathy, for Paris and it may be argued that they represented a desire to tighten the focus upon the lovers and increase the tempo of the scene. Curiously this ran counter to the mood of the rest of the scene, in which the director placed very heavy emphasis upon the other members of the Veronese society.

The actors fought against the contrived deaths that Bogdanov had planned for them and as a result the deaths retained their simplicity and curious lyric beauty, what Anne Pasternak Slater has aptly described as 'Petrarchanism come true'. Cusack's assessment of the moment of Juliet's death illustrates an actor's awareness that such moments draw strength from being played simply:

> The moment is simple, brief; there is no savouring of it, no making the dreadful grief and loss any deeper than it is. Just get it over with, finish numb: 'This is thy sheath; there rust, and let me die'.　　　　　　　(*Players of Shakespeare 2*, 1988, p. 125)

Juliet killed herself by placing Romeo's knife in his lifeless hands, holding it there with her own and then impaling herself upon it. This was a fine idea, which seemed to emphasize the close proximity of death and love that is one of the play's most important subtexts. It was, sadly, one of very few such moments, where a simple, relatively restrained action was used to underscore the text rather than to dominate it.

At that moment there was a brief blackout, and then Bogdanov came close to following the example of Peter Brook's 1947 production by cutting the rest of the play. However, where Brook had cut the lines in order to force the audience to leave the theatre with the final image of the violence of the deaths, Bogdanov had quite different ideas. After the blackout Bogdanov inserted the first twelve lines from the play's opening Chorus, which had been cut from the start of the play. This was altered into the past tense and spoken by the Prince but it is the circumstances in which the speech was delivered that demonstrate most clearly Bogdanov's manipulation of Shakespeare's emotionally complex ending. In place of the bier on which the dead bodies of Romeo and Juliet had previously sprawled, two life-sized golden statues stood upright on a raised plinth. This of course 'anticipates' Montague's promise to raise a 'statue in pure gold' to his daughter, a rather confusing visual reference, since the lines had been cut in this production. Photographers rushed forward from the audience to snap *paparazzi* pictures of the unveiling ceremony while the television cameras recorded the scene. A series of photo calls then ensued: a solo of Escalus, Montague and Capulet shaking hands, Lady Montague and Lady Capulet, the Nurse holding the rope ladder previously used by Romeo to gain access to Juliet's bedroom, the Friar and the Nurse, the Apothecary. The Prince then exited through the audience, pursued by the media.

In many ways this seemed to transform the scene into a display of supreme cynicism; tragedy turned into a media event in which everything and everybody becomes part of the media circus. In the desire to suggest the calculated exploitation of human suffering by the modern media Bogdanov had at the very least radically simplified Shakespeare's original. The result was theatrically effective, perhaps even in some respects laudable. Shakespeare's text certainly makes us aware of the inadequacy of response by those who remain after the lovers' deaths and arguably invites some revulsion at the way that the Prince expropriates the deaths in order to achieve civic order: 'Capulet, Montague,/See what a scourge is laid upon your hate. . . . Some shall be pardon'd and some punished . . .' (v iii 291–308). To see the conclusion in this way would undoubtedly constitute a modern distortion of the value of public rituals, but it would at least have some textual validity. However, Shakespeare's conclusion, like so much else in the play, represents a reconciliation of superficially incompatible emotions. Shakespeare was not merely preaching the orthodox view that out of much suffering may come some good. The long recapitulation by Friar Laurence and the almost ritualized acknowledgement of grief and guilt do not diminish the tragedy, nor do they compensate for it. In their inadequacy the survivors remind us of what is lost by those who, in Friar Laurence's phrase, love and live, moderately. Under Bogdanov's direction the play ended with audacious theatrical intensity and conceptual clarity often lacking in more conventional approaches. Ultimately however, it is not merely idolatry that justifies the retention of the final 100 lines of the play.

11   TERRY HANDS, RSC, 1989/90

This production originated in the Swan theatre, which had been created as a venue primarily for the work of Shakespeare's lesser-known contemporaries. The designer, Farrah, did little to interfere with the architectural simplicity of the theatre, with its bare wooden stage surrounded on three sides by an audience. Indeed, it is almost misleading to speak of a set design for this production at all. Farrah's single significant contribution was to place the branch of a weeping willow overhanging Juliet's balcony. The costumes were equally unobtrusive, with almost everyone dressed in beige and cream, so that it was almost impossible visually to distinguish the Capulets from the Montagues. Instead every change of mood and scene was achieved through lighting, often to striking effect. Two moments stood out for the subtle economy with which a mood of powerful lyricism was achieved. At the moment when Romeo and Juliet meet, the other guests at the ball were frozen in a warm amber glow, while the shared sonnet of the first exchange and the climactic kiss were picked out by a tight spotlight of white light. This is a device that had been used with similar success in Karolos Koun's 1967 production. By freezing the background action the director is able to capture the fleeting triumph over time that is central to the lovers' vow. The scene takes on something of the frozen intensity of a lightning flash and is then once again enveloped in the everyday bustle of the party. This is quite superior to the way that Zeffirelli had isolated the lovers by closing the main curtain in front of the party and staging the sonnet exchange in front of it in total isolation.

In the balcony scene the primary source of light was filtered through the willow leaves, dappling the stage and surrounding Juliet with a muted glow. The balcony of the Swan is perhaps seven metres above the stage, providing an unusually large distance between the two lovers. As had been the case in Zeffirelli's production, the extra distance had the great merit of making Romeo's inability to reach Juliet, and his subsequent need for a rope ladder, seem entirely convincing. In many productions Juliet's frustrated cry, 'What satisfaction canst thou have tonight' runs perilously close to comedy. Hands had apparently learned from his earlier experience in directing the 1973 production, in which Romeo climbed halfway up the stairs so that he could just touch Juliet's hand, leaving the audience to wonder why he did not simply take the last few steps. In 1989 the set and lighting did not make a mockery of the scene's lyricism, although the physical separation made the actors' task more difficult by reducing the intimacy of the scene.

Rylance and Slowe both looked the part of teenage lovers perfectly, and their performances, along with the production as a whole, achieved a unity almost unique in the modern history of this play. Rylance exhibited something of the brooding, introspective adolescence that he displayed in the part of Hamlet in the same season. He is physically small, with an expressive face best suited to studied melancholy and his voice, although rather light, is expressive and clear, despite his decision to play the part with a slight stammer in the early scenes. From the outset he seemed less an extravagant youth than a bookish introvert, always aware of the fragility of human expectations.

Georgia Slowe looked a perfect match, an utterly convincing teenager, given to demonstrations of eager, wide-eyed vitality. In the early scenes she seemed childish, almost fragile, despite her latent energy. Her apparent childishness was emphasized in her swift-footed movements, as she skipped round the room in her opening scenes and lent poignancy in later scenes as her parents continued to respond to surface appearance while missing her emerging reserve and maturity. Capulet's failure to recognize the alteration was particularly affecting when he announced his daughter's forthcoming marriage to Paris, hugging his little girl in joy and then, assuming that her rejection is childish coyness, chasing her round the room and spanking her in mock anger. Georgia Slowe's youth and inexperience meant that she was occasionally just short of meeting the challenge of the verse. This was particularly evident in her bedchamber anticipation of the terrors of the crypt, which she tried to treat almost as an operatic aria, projecting the horrors outward rather than internalizing them.

Overall, the central characters benefited at the expense of the supporting cast, especially the Nurse and Mercutio, from Hands's attempts to emphasize the play's unity of tone. David O'Hara's Mercutio used a Glaswegian accent to good effect in establishing the character as an outsider who survives by his wits. He was energetic and, when crossed, both threatening and unpredictable. He was particularly effective in conveying the character's sardonic wit, managing to suggest that his compulsive resort to sexual jokes masked vulnerability and fear of love. In II iv, his verbal attack upon the Nurse was accompanied by a hilariously energetic fumbling at her bottom that suggested barely constrained cruelty.

In the Queen Mab speech, O'Hara showed the character to be progressively infatuated by his own rhetoric, a bluff Scot who was suddenly discovering the depths of his own capacity for imaginative extravagance. At 'True, I talk of dreams/ Which are the children of an idle brain' (I iv 96–7), Mercutio was evidently regaining control over himself with a real effort of the will, a man slightly afraid of what he had revealed to others – and to himself – about his own unconscious mind. The performance lacked the exuberance sometimes associated with the character and his death was accompanied by a strangely muted stoicism rather than rage. However, it was consistent with the production's emphasis upon the central characters, and by controlling the impact of Mercutio's death the director avoided the loss of energy that sometimes accompanies the character's departure from the scene.

Margaret Courtenay's performance as the Nurse followed the traditional line of presenting the character as a solid, lower-class servant of ambiguous morality. In her encounters with Mercutio she rose to fine comic dignity, rejecting his advances with the scorn of a duchess and in her relationship with Juliet she managed to suggest a complex mixture of love and desire to see her charge marry advantageously. Physical warmth jostled against the shrewd calculations of a faithful retainer in an aristocratic household. Most important, despite the fact that the Nurse is a notoriously 'famous role', the great strength of Courtenay's approach was that it was always conceived as background to our understanding of Juliet.

If Hands sought unity by underplaying Mercutio and the Nurse, both characters who have unbalanced many a production, the loss was clearly a calculated one. There were other minor sacrifices resulting from the drive for artistic unity, particularly as there seemed little development in Romeo from the infatuation of the early scenes to his subsequent deeper love for Juliet. However, the directorial approach certainly allowed the eponymous characters to occupy the emotional heart of the production, suggesting a pair whose tragedy derived less from inexorable social pressures than from what Shakespeare shows to be an inextricable link between an all-consuming love and death. In its focus upon the central characters, its austere setting and its lack of superficial gaiety and bustle, the production pushed the poetry of the lovers' language into the foreground in a way that has certainly been all too often absent.

Hands was able to take advantage of the unlocalized nature of the bare stage by treating the three scenes of the final act as one continuous piece. It is often the case that a pause for scene changes distracts from the text's ironic juxtapositions: Juliet lies apparently dead but ready to wake into her husband's arms; Romeo eagerly anticipates 'joyful news at hand' but is about to hear of death. In this production, Juliet was left in shadow on the stage, while the musicians bantered with Peter a few feet away. The bedroom was then transformed into the family tomb by simply placing metal gates across the upstage gap between the pillars that supported the balcony. With the main stage shrouded in darkness Romeo appeared in bright light above on the balcony. The narrow separation of life from death, comedy from tragedy, and the distance of Verona from Mantua were all indicated by using one of the play's most pervasive images, that of light and dark, in the contrast between the shadow of the tomb and sunlight above on the balcony.

Rylance exhibited perhaps too much of his earlier melancholy in his long speech over Juliet's body, and the scene lacked much of the poignancy and romantic ardour implicit in the text. Instead it was treated as a dirge, extracting every scrap of grief from the lines. Rylance is an actor who balances a fine, intelligent sensitivity to the lines with a tendency to over-internalize them, resulting in a rather monotonous delivery. His death scene lacked emotional variety even if it held the audience's attention to the lines.

As had been the case in the 1976 production, the final lines of the play gained much from the presence of a fine, raw-nerved Capulet, here played by Bernard Horsefall. As with the earlier production, Capulet was portrayed as a domestic tyrant, likely at any moment to erupt into violence to maintain command. This was especially evident early in the play, at the party in his home. In order to gain temporary control over Tybalt during his heated exchange over Tybalt's desire to challenge Romeo, Capulet abruptly and quite brutally slapped Tybalt across the face. There was to be no doubt who was master here. Again as with the 1976 production, by establishing the violence of the character his collapse gave the final moments an emotional focus. Interestingly, Hands retained Montague's reference to the sudden death of his wife from grief at her son's banishment. The retention of this line is relatively rare in modern productions; it is often cut on the grounds that it distracts attention unnecessarily from a proper focus upon the central deaths. However, here it served its proper function by helping to build the larger pattern of the ending in which the audience is made increasingly aware of the full social context of the private tragedy.

The final scene also gained in intensity from the fact that the tensions between Montague and Capulet were clearly not easily resolved. Even with the dead bodies of their children before them the lesson was almost ignored. Even as Montague confronted the dead bodies with a cry of anguish, Capulet crossed over to Juliet's prostrate body to extract the knife. Servants reached for their swords as Capulet seemed about to renew the fight but the Prince's command to seal up the tomb brought a collapse that showed that this last vestige of the feud came more from ancient habit than from new anger. Instead the play ended with the Friar, Montague and Capulet all kneeling beside the bier on which Juliet and Romeo lay. Montague and Capulet then reached across the dead bodies to join hands in a simple but effective final tableau.

12   GENERAL CONCLUSIONS

Shakespeare is not our contemporary, nor does he write plays that conform strictly to the pattern of classical Greek tragedy.

Of course it does not necessarily follow that in *Romeo and Juliet* we may not discover aspects that seem to indicate tragic character flaws in the eponymous hero and heroine. And there is quite clearly much about the play that is instantly recognizable to a contemporary audience. However, a number of the difficulties faced by critic and director alike in coming to terms with this play arise more or less directly from one or two key areas where theatrical conventions or social attitudes have significantly changed over the centuries.

There can be little doubt, for instance, that modern audiences find the public demonstrations of grief that end the play rather hard to accept: we seem to demand spontaneous emotion and we are suspicious of any reconciliation that is expressed through the medium of ritual or formal rhetoric. It is a truism of any production of any of Shakespeare's plays that it will fall short of an ideal; this is part of the ephemeral pleasure of the theatre as well as one of the difficulties in staging works that have received such universal and minute scrutiny, as well as having been performed with such frequency. However, *Romeo and Juliet* has a claim to be considered as a special case, both for the challenge of the final act and for the extraordinary nature of its verse. I suspect that modern audiences may well be less attuned than Shakespeare's original auditors to complexity based on verbal nuance and paradox, just as we are more demanding of a play's visual impact. If this is true, then every modern production of *Romeo and Juliet* will necessarily be a compromise between the demands of word and image.

Theatrical solutions have had varied success. Michael Bogdanov's production, which I have described as deeply flawed, nonetheless represents one logical extreme in its attempt to 'translate' every Elizabethan theatrical and social convention into a thoroughly modern idiom. In this respect it is closely akin to *West Side Story*. Few who saw it failed to respond strongly, one way or another. 'Translation' of one sort or another was attempted in most of the other productions; ranging from Zeffirelli's attempts systematically to find visual images corresponding to each of the most significant textual images, to the inclusion of a life-size doll in the 1973 production in an attempt to convey the excesses of Mercutio's imagination. At best such directorial decisions have provoked a significant re-assessment of the play, as was the case with Zeffirelli's production, which conclusively demonstrated the vitality of the play's youthful passions.

The problem of casting the central characters remains particularly challenging. Certainly the evidence of recent productions confirms the view that Romeo and Juliet must be thought of as a pair, to be cast together rather than as distinct individuals. The time the characters spend together on stage is so limited that the audience must instantly be convinced of their all-consuming love; otherwise the production must become unbalanced.

No production has yet achieved a full success with the final scene; perhaps it represents a theatrical tradition that is now out of tune with modern attitudes. On the other hand, the relative success of the 1989 RSC production may indicate that venues such as the Swan theatre, which impose a relatively simple production style, may in a sense make the audience more receptive to the play's language and some of its more ritualistic staging. Ultimately I would argue that this is the only way that anything like an ideal production will be achieved; by the same token, the current conventions of film must inevitably produce a version of the play that substitutes image for word and thereby reduces even further Shakespeare's endeavours. Charles Gildon, writing in 1710, is perhaps the earliest critic to record and question the curious relationship that exists in *Romeo and Juliet* between passion and verbal dexterity:

> Whether Passion be so pregnant of Similes as Romeo and Juliet everywhere give us I dare not determine, since to say that all they speak is not natural wou'd be to provoke too many that admire it as the Soul of Love.
> (Reprinted in B. Vickers, ed. *Shakespeare: the Critical Heritage*, vol. 2, p. 254)

Gildon's reservations apply at least as forcefully today but the director or critic who tries to ignore or minimize this relationship cannot truly be said fully to have confronted the play as Shakespeare wrote it.

READING LIST

The most useful editions are T. J. B. Spencer (ed.), New
Penguin Shakespeare (1967); G. Blakemore Evans (ed.), New
Cambridge Shakespeare (1984) and Brian Gibbons (ed.),
New Arden Shakespeare (1980). Evans provides useful information and illustrations about a number of early productions.
One final edition, by Neil King (ed.), in the Illustrated
Shakespeare Series (Stanley Thorne, Cheltenham, 1989) deserves mention, not for its presentation of the text, but for the
inclusion of photographs and illustrations from 33 different
productions of the play, including most of those covered in
this book.

CRITICAL ESSAYS

The field of criticism is cursorily surveyed in Neil Taylor and
Bryan Loughrey (eds), *Shakespeare's Early Tragedies* (Macmil-
lan Casebook, 1990). The selection includes extracts from
some of the criticism listed below, as well as extracts from
early critics of the play. A more comprehensive guide to the
range of criticism of the play is provided by Stanley Wells
(ed.), *The Cambridge Companion to Shakespeare Studies* (1986).
   Other studies include:
Nicholas Brooke, Shakespeare's Early Tragedies (London,
   Methuen, 1968).
Harry Levin, 'Form and Formality in *Romeo and Juliet*' in
   Shakespeare and the Revolution of the Times (Oxford Univer-
   sity Press, 1976).
Ann Pasternak Slater, 'Petrarchanism come true in *Romeo and
   Juliet*' in Werner Habicht, D. J. Palmer and Roger Pringle
   (eds), *Images of Shakespeare* (Associated University Presses,
   London, 1988).

Susan Snyder, *The Comic Matrix in Shakespeare's Tragedies* (Princeton University Press, Princeton NJ, 1979).

Stanley Wells, 'Juliet's Nurse: the uses of inconsequentiality' in Philip Edwards, Inga-Stina Ewbank and G. K. Hunter (eds), *Shakespeare's Styles* (Cambridge University Press, 1980).

PERFORMANCE

Performance history is surveyed briefly in both the New Arden and New Cambridge editions. George C. D. Odell, *Shakespeare from Betterton to Irving* (Dover Publications, New York, 1966) provides an invaluable survey of eighteenth and nineteenth-century productions. Jill L. Levenson, *Romeo and Juliet*, Shakespeare in Performance Series (Manchester University Press, 1987) covers productions by Garrick, Gielgud, Peter Brook and Zeffirelli (stage and film), as well as providing speculation on the Elizabethan production. Further information may be found in the following:

John Russell Brown, 'S. Franco Zeffirelli's *Romeo and Juliet*', *Shakespeare Survey*, XV, 1962, reprinted in *Shakespeare's Plays in Performance* (Harmondsworth, 1969).

Philip Brockbank (ed.), *Players of Shakespeare* (Cambridge, 1985), (contains material on performing the Nurse, by Brenda Bruce).

Gareth Lloyd Evans, 'Judi Dench talks to Gareth Lloyd Evans' in *Shakespeare Survey*, XXVII, 1974 (covers the Zeffirelli production of 1961).

Russell Jackson and Robert Smallwood (eds), *Players of Shakespeare 2* (Cambridge University Press, 1988), (articles by Roger Allam on acting Mercutio and Niamh Cusack on acting Juliet).

INDEX OF NAMES